Two
Brothers
a bit of a yarn

Two
Brothers
a bit of a yarn
by Roger Furphy

Primavera
SYDNEY

© Roger Furphy 1996
© Primavera 1996

CIP
Furphy, Roger 1940 -
Two brothers: a bit of a yarn

ISBN 1 875368 29 9

1. Furphy, Joseph, 1843-1912. 2. Furphy, John, 1842-1920.
3. Authors, Australian - Biography. 4. Novelists, Australian - Biography.
5. Blacksmiths Victoria - Biography. I. Title.

994.030922

Furphy

John Furphy was the maker of the horse-drawn water and sanitary carts that serviced the Anzac camps in Melbourne and later in the Middle East during World War I. The carts' mobility meant that their drivers became the carriers of rumours and false stories, and this gave rise to the expression's current meaning.

A family name became a brand name became an Australian colloquialism.

Contents

Preface

Great-grandfathers and other relatives from the past seem less remembered in our Australian culture these days than they used to be. We do not have in our living rooms portraits of ancestors staring down at us with noble demeanour and the expectation that we will carry on their traditions—though such portraits still adorn the walls of schools and boardrooms. And we do not cite the example of what Great-Grandfather Henry did to impel us to action now.

I have often pondered the reason for this. It cannot be that the pace of Australian society gives us little time to reflect, for society lives at a hectic pace everywhere. Perhaps it is simply that in the dynamism of the present, which is the flavour of society nowadays, the traditions and continuity represented by these ancestors are no longer important. We have too much that is immediate to be concerned with, and we see ourselves as individuals making our own way rather than members of a family or institution carried along by the stream of custom.

And yet this great-grandfather and his brother have continually tapped at my consciousness. Having owned and worked the Furphy Foundry three generations later, I have found that there have been times when I felt close to both these men. The story of the origin of my foundry fascinates me, as does the difference between my great-grandfather John and his famous brother Joseph.

I have felt that the brothers wanted to tell me their side of the story. But divulging inner thoughts was not the done thing in their day—not for men anyway. In their different ways, they kept their mouths buttoned and their feelings under cover. So I have had to imagine what went on in their hearts.

And so with the main events in the lives of these two men I found myself filling in the gaps. In my imagination I have over the years honed the details of their lives, until these details became reality to me, though they must remain fiction to the reader. John and Joe are part of my heritage, even part of my being, and I have felt inclined to the liberty of weaving a story around what we know of their lives. Some of my liberties, in particular Joe's love affair with Kate, are stories that have been knocking around my family down the generations, so this has an authority of a kind.

Others have published much about Joseph Furphy from the more usual kind of authority: surviving letters and documents. Their account of him is accurate in the academic sense, but I doubt it is what Joe would have wanted to read. His nature seems more disposed to invention and a good yarn. John, his opposite in nature, was made as bosses and men of stature have to be—practical, zealous, impatient of fools, but yet caught up in the tensions inherent in his puritan religion. The brothers were as unalike as Jacob and Esau, the one taking after his father, the other after his mother, as in the biblical story. So my story is about the tensions between two such classically different brothers.

I would like to thank Trish Frost for encouraging me to go on when I showed her the first few pages.

CHAPTER I

The BOSS and the Bullocky

THE LITTLE PICKET gate swung open freely. Oiled the night before, it had gradually softened its will to hold and creak in the early morning light. Joe walked down the narrow path lined with the untidy canes of gnarled old rose bushes, and onto the footpath. In the deep earthen gutter at the edge of the road the protruding waste pipes from the row of cottages poured out their small flow of warm effluent, the vapour dissipating quickly in the cold July air.

It reminded Joe of a different smell: the aroma of bullocks, the strength of the vapour from their nostrils lingering on crisp morning—the smell of life. The contrast was overwhelming and Joe pondered the two extremes as he walked to his brother's foundry. The small town, spreading its young urban branches but unable to reach past its own growth to the open space and clean air beyond. Bullocks heaving in unison, their strong bodies defying the load they pulled, each day making new ground.

As he turned into the main street the foundry whistle

speared the low, soft fog with a sharp burst that released a jet of steam and could be heard all over the town. Like a starter's gun, for many it heralded the start of work for yet another day. He would be late by five minutes or so, but he preferred it this way, thus avoiding his brother's morning ritual of job allocation and the usual comment on yesterday's work that inevitably referred to the time taken for individual jobs rather than the quality of workmanship.

Joe's work was slow but methodical, and he knew that the pace of his other, preferred work of bullock-driving influenced his foundry work: cautious and correct like the straining bullocks, and seemingly in no hurry to rid himself of his daily load. He was, as some had remarked, a plodder, tall, thin, with a slight stoop. His coat appeared to weigh heavily on him, like fresh rain weighing down the new growth of a climbing rose. His face was drawn, his cheeks hollowed.

Outside the foundry a small footbridge from the roadway to the footpath was the crossing place for those who rode bicycles to work. Their tyremarks made small snake-like lines in the soft earth. Two particular lines stood out: deeper, straighter, with a series of squares that gave a chequered pattern, fading at its edges. Joe guessed that John had been at work for at least an hour. Ben, the blacksmith's rouseabout, had also started early. His first job was to light the three forges, and so when Joe entered the small front section of the shop the warm phosphorus smell of burning coke was as welcome as the smells of a good cooking stove. Inside the front door, on one side, a small office with pigeonhole windows protruded into the work area. John was seated and beckoned to Joe.

John was a big man, shorter than Joe but heavier and stronger, and distinguished-looking, his white beard neatly trimmed, his eyes blue and bright. His waistcoat stretched somewhat around an abundant torso; the gold chain holding the front flaps tightly against his stomach could not conceal a middle-aged spread. Joe remembered a walnut tree on the way to the foundry, its ageing fruit splitting open its outer jacket—no restraint there, but rather a need to make its presence felt. He hoped that their discussion could open with the frankness they had had between them as children and young men.

Five minutes later and the pair were sitting at the bench that surrounded the walls of the inner office. Joe was taking instructions on a trip to Melbourne, a journey that would see him accompany John's latest invention, a grain-stripper, to the Centennial Exhibition. It was arranged that Joe would haul the stripper to Seymour, fifty miles south of Shepparton, using two bullocks. At Seymour he would link up with the latest mode of transport, steam rail, for the journey further south.

John needed another four weeks to get his prize exhibit ready, and so the end of April was set as the date for the trip. This suited Joe. It would give him precious days to complete some stories in time for the *Bulletin*'s competition. The thought of hand-delivering his entries, with the possibility of witnessing the adjudication and announcement of the winner, the thought of discussing and deliberating with other writers—all this would be exciting indeed.

Joe opened the door of the office and they stepped down onto the foundry floor. John was still speaking, a contented glint in his eyes. Joe's mind had wandered to his *Bulletin* entries, and when John called he turned, but the noise of the steam hammers drowned out what was said. Joe waved and gave a half-grin, not sure of the appropriate response.

Today was tines day. The constant banging of light-gauge steel strips would produce hundreds of comb-like tines that would be fitted to the front of the grain-stripper, their job to accept the grain stem in some order so that the head stood ready for a clean cut. Joe's job was the last operation on what was a small assembly line. It started with a 27-inch strip of steel two inches wide, heated to a red-orange colour in the open forge and passed with tongs to the hammer operator, who bevelled and pointed the steel into shape.

The final operation was for Joe to punch two square bolt holes at the blunt end that would allow for fastening to the stripper. A frame or jig was placed over a set of six tines. Markings indicated the area to locate the punch; a timed strike with a four-pound hammer drove the punch through in one blow. That was the secret—two blows were twice the effort. Joe rarely missed a blow, and if he did it would have been because of the operation slowing down up the line, allowing the steel to cool and harden. From the glowing hot steel momentarily arching as if in spasm as the punch penetrated it, its colour would change to a dull reddish grey.

Joe positioned himself at the bench, set a row of six tines in line and manoeuvred the jig. The team was under way. As the routine set in, his mind turned to another team, a team of bullocks working under considerably better conditions, a different heat, the quiet surroundings of the bush, the lingering but subdued, distant call of a crow.

The same whistle that signalled the start of the day sounded at the end, but this time a little longer as if celebrating the cessation of work. The foundry slowed. Thirty minutes elapsed before old Don the blacksmith bent to fasten his bicycle clips; it had taken time to place tools in position for the morning and gather a bucket of kindling in readiness for lighting the forge. The bike wobbled as Don's old legs pushed at the pedals, then gathered speed as he sailed off. Don lived with his spinster sisters, each week handing over his pay packet to them. They cooked his

16

meals, went shopping each day, and brought back snippets of gossip that either went over the top of Don's head or joined a backlog of verbal hysteria that sat cached somewhere in the back of his brain, never to be deciphered.

Apart from Don, the sisters' main interest was cleaning and maintaining the small Wesleyan church directly across the street from their house. There was no full-time minister, but John Furphy was the principal lay preacher. Don and his sisters were fervent parishioners. The sisters inclined to almost worship Don's boss, Don himself finding a common interest other than work to share with John. But the foundry was Don's life, and when he arrived home that evening the ache in his arms and shoulders signalled the end of another rewarding day.

John enjoyed this time of the day. He had checked to see that Don's bike was not in its usual position. The foundry was empty. There was time to inspect the day's work, to check the leather belts that turned numerous pulleys, stretching under load. This was the time to take up the slack, re-riveting the leather into its new position. Today, however, a more important task awaited him, that of selecting the component parts that would make up the new height adjustment mechanism for the grain-stripper, an addition that would surely impress the judges enough to declare his brainchild the winner.

John walked to the far end of the foundry. The casting area looked neat and shipshape. The black earthen floor, covered with rows of sand moulds, resembled a small cemetery full of infant graves. Shafts of late afternoon sun had found openings in the western wall and created an eerie haze above the moulds, some of which were still emitting a steamy smoke. The pour had taken place that afternoon. The moulds prepared over the preceding days had accepted the molten iron, which now assumed their inner shape. They would cool overnight, to be broken open in the morning.

John bent over one of the moulds. He needed to see that the pour had been successful before the rest were opened. He removed the overfill, which had created a pattern of thin iron sections joined by larger blobs. He hesitated before separating the mould, then slowly lifted the cope from the drag. Inside two cogs lay side by side, one larger than the other, and joined by a runner that had directed the molten iron through the sand, an umbilical cord to be discarded. He adjusted his glasses, kneeling down for a closer inspection. Easing the castings from the sand, he tapped them lightly so that the sand fell away, revealing the smooth grey skin of the perfectly formed castings. They would become the main components of the self-adjusting mechanism. Other blacksmiths might have toyed with the same idea. Indeed there was talk of an American machine with a similar capability about to be imported, but John knew he had the edge; his casting facility gave him the jump on them all. Placing the cogs on a metal tray, he returned to his office. The light was fading. Just time to run the callipers over the critical dimensions before locking up for the day.

Joe's spare time was taken up by his writing, if not at home then at the Shepparton Mechanics' Institute and Library, a combined institution within walking distance of their cottage. The separate place and time he made for his writing expressed the estrangement that was growing between him and his wife. The long periods when Joe was away bullock-driving had affected what little companionship they had had. Leonie had ceased to grieve, accepting that her life would be lonely. Only her children gave her reason to feel wanted. She found it more and more easy to say little to her husband.

Joe stood, easing his back as he walked from the kitchen to a small shed he had built at the rear of the cottage, set in a garden that sloped to the banks of the Goulburn River.

This was his 'sanctum', Joe's name for his private writing room. It was nothing flash, just corrugated iron and slab walls but with a fine view of the river and its red gums. The clutter of books around a large armchair, the desk and type-writer and the kerosene lamp shaded by an old hat gave it an atmosphere of warmth that he needed to set him at ease for writing. He had bought the typewriter, only the third writing machine in Shepparton, to try and get his long and unwieldy manuscript, *Such Is Life*, into shape. But now he was writing some verses for publication in the *Bulletin*.

Five hours later Joe stood and reached to turn down the oil lamp, the thumb and the forefinger large and clumsy around the delicate brass fittings. He had reread the verse several times before embarking on the final draft. He was satisfied it could not be improved on, only added to. But this might make it a bit boring, and besides, a limit of five hundred words was a condition of publication. All that remained was to write a letter of introduction. Darkness came as Joe left the shed. His mind raced through the memorised verse of 'The Gum-sucker's Dirge'.

> *Better we were cold and still, with our famous Jim and Bill,*
> *Beneath the interdicted wattle-bough,*
> *For the angels made our date five-and-twenty years too late,*
> *And there is no Up the Country for us now.*

In the cottage Leonie had prepared supper. By now her instinct seemed able to determine the precise time that Joe would appear. Some nights his mood was better than others, and tonight he was unusually communicative. Sam and Felix had gone to bed. At ten and twelve years respectively, they were growing fast. Leonie had for some time now wished to talk of their future. She resented Joe's inability to show concern for their well-being, particularly when he continually mentioned his parents' teaching skills and the care and guidance they gave him and John. They talked about it, and as always Leonie regretted mentioning it, for it induced a feeling of guilt in Joe and undermined what manly feeling he did have of duty towards his family. After all he did provide for them, hard and all as it was with his long trips away and his writing.

He promised that when he returned from Melbourne he would devote his time to them continually until their immediate future was worked out. The way he said it convinced Leonie that he would. And later, in their separate beds, sleep came to them in different ways. Leonie, content, knowing that Joe always kept his promise and always excelled at achieving when he put his mind to it, gave herself up to the heavy sleep that swept in on her.

Joe lay long awake. His mind kept returning to the verse, lingering on the lines 'that there is no Up the Country for us now'. He remembered his boyhood around Kangaroo Ground, the small clearings they called farms, with the virgin bush all around. There was still 'Up the Country' for him, and by Jove there would be for his sons.

Flattener

CHAPTER 2

Samuel and Judith

HE TWO BROTHERS turned and waved to their mother. John's wave was decisive, practised, the first of many disciplined movements that would follow throughout the day at the small country school. He had moved on ahead. Joe was still beside his mother, who had walked with them the one and a half miles to the Yering school.

'Thanks Mum for taking the low track,' he whispered, just in case John was within hearing distance. His mother's gentle smile remained in his vision as he turned quickly; then faded as he gained momentum, running now to catch his older brother.

Judith returned to the cottage along the high track—apart from being the shortest way, the trees and scrub here were less dense. The sun cast long shafts of bright light, picking out the the subtle colours of tree-trunks, their clear grey skin, and some long strands of bark hanging loose, or wedged between trunk and limb. Fallen leaves, dried and hardened, appeared to retain life with a warmth of soft colour. Rosellas winged then glided their way through the tall timber in bursts of red and blue.

The low track followed Cambell's Creek. Thick scrub and bracken lined the winding path; wild blackberry bushes broke ranks as their thorny leaders reached to secure a hold, like human arms reaching over barricades at a street parade, touching and clasping all that passed by. The rain overnight had swollen the creek, which moved faster, its normal gentle sound now a mild roar. Judith knew their clothes would get wet as they brushed past the ferns, that the low track was longer and wetter under foot, but she and her sons also knew that after rain there was a very good chance they'd see old Rufus the wallaby.

Unlike the kangaroos that mysteriously appeared at the cottage garden in large numbers early morning and evenings, Rufus usually stayed hidden in the dense scrub, a jet-black marsupial with rounded back and a neck that tapered to a small head with beady eyes. Sometimes they heard him crashing his way through the undergrowth, clumsily, without the kangaroo's grace in motion. They had named him after the village cobbler, a hunchback with a short neck and wire-framed glasses on the end of his nose.

John was more interested in getting where he was going, and wished they'd taken the high track that Judith was now returning on. Since the rain that night John had anticipated Joe's request and so at breakfast he was first to bags the high track. Judith noticed how premeditated, calculating this had been. John was growing up, and so Judith had decided to favour the younger and more susceptible, as mothers usually do.

Judith was now clear of the bush. Semi-cleared paddocks, wooden fences, some pigs, a cow, a winding road—harsh, hard and dry even after the rain, and she knew it would never look like Ireland with its greener grass and stone fences, but she didn't really care any more.

It was eight years since they had arrived at Port Phillip on the *Argyle* from Ireland. Judith was seventeen, Samuel twenty-two. At sixteen Judith Murphy had eloped from Artmore and her parish church, whose spire was built by her grandfather Robert Murphy in 1780. The church was vacant the day they married at Lurgan to the north in the Presbyterian church, and three weeks later sailed for Australia. They left Ireland for two main reasons: to search for a more prosperous life and to escape the misery of their ancestral and religious differences.

Ironically, it was on an occasion steeped in sectarian bigotry that they had met. It was a weekend at Keady, a small village outside Artmore. Judith was with five of her closest school friends, all Catholics. Sunday afternoon was a time to congregate in the shopping centre after Mass. On this Sunday, however, the annual picnic procession of the local branch of the Royal Ulster Brigade was making its way through the streets towards the girls.

Four narrow streets wound their way down to a town square flanked by the more prominent shops and commercial establishments. The girls were standing just around the corner, close to a wall that protected them from a cold easterly wind and absorbed the thin winter sun into its red bricks. Like cats in an alley, they had found a place to settle, to laze, from which to observe.

As the marching Orangemen came to the corner that led into the square Judith noticed mainly their age, which varied from youngsters of fourteen years to fathers and grandfathers. Each wore a wide orange sash that crossed their chests and fastened at their sides, forming a vivid backdrop to their silver and gold instruments. Suddenly there was a loss of momentum. The music faltered, and it was not for several more embarrassing steps that the musicians realised that their bass drum had fallen silent. They were now in the square, where small supporting groups had gathered to be strengthened by the solidarity and pageantry of the occasion. They stopped, and all turned as one to see their bass drummer unclipping his huge drum from its heavy leather harness. Slowly he held back a gaping wound to the hide of his drum, then reaching into its innards, removed a two-inch lump of road metal. His face changed to a red rage as he held up the murderous object with one arm and with the other pointed to a group of girls scattering, one of them still clinging to a slingshot.

Judith had hesitated, while the other girls ran off. She enjoyed watching the confusion, but then as the band members looked in her direction she started to run too, soon catching up with her friends. Now the girls stopped, frightened. Like a herd of young fallow deer their heads turned anxiously, looking for a leader, panic in their eyes. Then they scattered, each running for herself.

Judith turned into an alley. There was light at the end—she would not be trapped. But an arm was around her waist, supple like a lion's paw. She was caught. Turning quickly, she looked straight into Samuel's blue eyes. There was no anger there. He smiled, then released her. That was how they met.

Now ten years on, Judith had hardened to the new country. As the young eucalypt saplings that appeared to defy the harsh dry ground by propagating, spreading their young limbs under this southern sun, she too with her husband was rearing a young family. There was a warm feeling of security, a sense of moving ahead, achievement. The warmth in Ireland was of a different kind, for there with family and friends you closed in, held on, to maintain a standard that somehow now didn't seem worth holding to. As she turned the latch to enter their small cottage she waved to Millie, a friend whose cottage was identical and whose husband James was employed with Samuel to work the Anderson farm.

Old Anderson was a good boss. His farm was considered by many the best in the district. It was fourteen miles to the east of La Trobe's village of Melbourne, which was now spreading in all directions, with a population that seemed to double every year—a busy port, with sailing ships arriving from Europe every few days. Anderson had often thought of his good luck the day he decided to visit the ships in order to hire men to work his farm. On this particular day, about two years before, the Argyle had just berthed after its long voyage from Dublin and Plymouth.

On that bright morning the scene was one of both anxiety and happiness. The seventy or eighty new arrivals on board were easily outnumbered by those waiting on the pier, many of whom, like Anderson, were waiting to select labour. Men, women, and even the older children could sense the scrutiny as they scrambled down the gangplank. The stronger men were claimed quickly, and so it took some time before Samuel and Judith were approached. Anderson had moved forward and with one hand tapped Samuel's shoulder; with the other he lifted his hat to Judith. After ten minutes or so of conversation and Anderson's description of his property and the sort of work it required, all seemed pleased and the newcomers had found a home.

There was, however, one condition that Samuel had insisted on: his good friend James Hunter, who had not yet appeared on deck, was also seeking work, and the two had decided to stick together, at least for the time being. Anderson had nodded his approval, though he wondered about hiring sight unseen. This quickly evaporated when Samuel waved and called to a man who had appeared at the top of the gangplank.

Even from that distance Anderson could see the strength in the man; the large coat he wore, stretched across the shoulder and chest, obviously concealed a power within. His broad face acknowledging Samuel's call was calm in the milling boisterous crowd as he turned and and waved down to them. Yes, Anderson had often considered that finding Hunter was the break that gave his farm a start on the others. It turned out that Hunter was an experienced blacksmith and had a knowledge of the latest farm implements used across Europe.

The voyage on board the *Argyle* was lonely and arduous for Samuel and Judith until they met the Hunters. Because men and women were segregated to separate sleeping quarters fore and aft of the ship, Samuel and his new bride had found privacy by day in the clinker hull of one of the six lifeboats that lined the ship's sides. Each boat was covered with a heavy canvas, and the two aftermost boats were secluded from view by the raised decking of the steering area. Old sailcloth doubled, and doubled again, and spread over the curved inner ribs of the boat, created a nest at sea. It was a secret hideaway too good to be true. The risk, the anxiety of clambering aboard unseen heightened the physical passion that usually followed.

Samuel had often referred to his son John as a 'child of the sea', and it was not until John became a young man that he thought he understood what his Dad had meant.

On one calm morning, close to midday, they were spotted as they entered the lifeboat. A message was quickly sent to the Captain. They were both ordered to duties in the ship's galley. James and Millie were there too, as it turned out for a similar offence though one less subtle, for James had simply made his way to the women's quarters to be with Millie.

The pitch and roll of the *Argyle* transmitted the ocean's depth, its unending power and supple movement. The tiny sailing ship, as fragile as a leaf twirling on a turbulent river, rode the vast mass that surged beneath it, safe in its oneness with its element. Samuel reflected on this as he rode the sharp jolt and clatter of Anderson's lorry, which cut its own demands on the hard, dry earth beneath it. It was a vehicle very much in control, with two strong horses answering to Anderson's commands. The four of them sat with Anderson, the two women behind the men and behind them a supply of goods for the farm: flour, salt, sugar, oils, soap, wire and other hardware. They were headed east, twenty miles or so. The opportunity to stock up, trading at keen prices around the docks area, was an opportunity Anderson had considered days before.

The road narrowed, and as they rounded the hills on their way to Kangaroo Ground they looked back on the tiny port town of Melbourne, with its tents and shanties, its bustling trade, the movement of people creating a halo of dust from the unmade streets, new people in a new country, refreshed, anxious with new hope, so vastly different from Ireland, whose solid buildings and fertile land were owned by so few.

The small farms were now interspersed with clusters of bush, bracken and huge eucalypts, then larger farms in the valleys. Anderson's was one of these, bordered on the far side by a fast-flowing river, the main house nearby and a row of cottages to one side. Samuel and Judith were dropped by a cottage. James, always obliging, carried their trunk from the lorry to the door while Anderson pointed to an oil lamp that hung by the door. James and Millie, who had admitted to Anderson they were not married, would spend time at the main house on domestic duties, each a chaperone for their respective gender.

In the eight years that followed, Samuel and Judith had worked hard, and become well liked by neighbours in the district. James and Millie were now well and truly married.

They had no children and Samuel had told Judith he thought they tried too hard—their light would blink out early each evening. The opposite had occurred with them. John was born only two months after their arrival, and Joseph ten months later. It was in their fourth year at Anderson's, when Judith had walked young John and Joe along Cambell's Creek to the schoolhouse and returned on the high track to their cottage on the farm, that Judith accepted that she must be pregnant again. She knew the first hidden signs: the dull ache, the secret anxiety that would lead to an utter contentment, and then back again into anxiety. She decided she would tell Samuel that night.

The evenings in the Furphy cottage lingered into the night. Judith was a teacher and the nights were precious times to encourage their children to read and write, but mainly to read. Their books were the Bible, poetry, Shakespeare, and at quite an early age the boys knew long passages by heart. Judith had hoped to teach at the children's school but realised now that she would have to wait, yet again, until her third child was born.

John and Joe were quick to learn. They had skipped two grades at school in as many years. Joe found a need to play with those of his own age. John on the other hand took to the promotion and those who went with it, finding the older boys and girls a challenge. Joe was able to write verses to the extent that his mother would read them, and sometimes reread them, and then even memorise them, so that the gentle innocence would come back to her as she lay awake at night.

On the low track Rufus lay.
 Sleeping by day,
Yet not happy to stay,
 'Cause it's mum's and my way.

Drill Hammer

CHAPTER 3

Childhood Lessons

ANDERSON'S FARM was by now the most prosperous in the district, and had a flourishing side business in the manufacture of farm implements. Hunter had indeed been a good find, a very profitable addition to the farm. His skills in blacksmithing allowed Anderson to take the designs of the latest implements brought out from America and adjust them to suit a harsher soil.

The blacksmith shop was relocated near the main gate and close to the road, thus allowing greater access to the increasing number of customers. Two rows of four forges heated iron bars to a dull orange colour; large hammers then thumped the iron into plastic shapes. Like hammers on a piano, not in unison, they delivered a sound of satisfaction for those who understood the degree of lift, the power of the downswing, and the dying hiss of the greying metal as it was plunged into water troughs.

Samuel often worked with Hunter at the blacksmith's shop when wet weather set in or when asked to help because of a backlog of orders. He enjoyed the co-operation, the discipline and the pace of the men working together under the tin roof.

After school and before supper John and Joe would often appear at the open doorway to watch their father. The nearest forge was about fifteen feet away. If only they were allowed closer! On some days they were able to sidestep across to and behind a heap of bagged coke, but only when the supply was stacked high enough. On those occasions they could see the orange iron flatten, then bend, then be tapped into the most delicate curves, hooks and circles—lasting impressions, strong and useful, unlike the insubstantial circles and squares written up in chalk and so easily wiped away.

At night after supper John would sit close by his father. The familiar dank smell of burnt coke and sweat in his flannel singlet indicated a day worked in the blacksmith shop—just a stale damp kind of mint odour, so different from the rank smell of his farm clothes. And so the questioning followed the appropriate day: the various iron components, their function when fitted to the implement, and the degree of draw on a section of steel rod tapered so that the thickest section of iron was where the greatest force would occur. Although his father was tired, his arms and shoulders sore, he told John all he knew. Neither parent ever denied their children any knowledge they could pass on.

Joe was more likely to be with his mother, learning poetry and stories from old Ireland, listening to her read and then comment, as if all she read required her criticism. Joe found this annoying because it slowed the flow of the story, but he nevertheless found some satisfaction in her ability to ponder the power of expression, and in later life a sentence or line and her comment on it would lift itself into his memory.

As well as the implement works, there was one other unique speciality of Anderson's farm, that of growing and selling fresh vegetables. Ming-To and his wife Tan worked with Millie around the main house, but the backyard sloping gently to the creek was their labour of love: the rich soil, irrigated by Ming's 'walking' waterwheel, yielded good crops of carrots, potatoes, spinach and corn. In the peak season a weekly load was carted to the street markets of Melbourne.

The Chinese couple had headed in the wrong direction in their search for gold. Ming-To would often think back to those frantic days on arrival at Melbourne. With little knowledge of English, he found from observing the departing groups that most European immigrants appeared to be headed north-west. But a smaller group of more affluent immigrants of Scottish and English descent were setting out to the north-east. Small groups of Chinese interspersed their ranks, small and bent with the weight of their loads, as if destined to become lackeys to the tall, straight backs of the regimented Scots. In their confusion Ming-To and Tan had attached themselves to these confident-looking strangers.

Their gold finds turned out to be few and far between. The gold lay deep in rock, quartz that speared a path into the flinty substance as if jackhammered by a thousand lightning strikes. It was not till months later that word spread across the country of the massive finds of mainly alluvial gold in the north-west of the colony.

On their way, headed back to Melbourne town, they had stopped off at Anderson's farm hoping to find some work. Somewhere to prop for a time, while Tan could give birth, away from the noise, dust and crude orders of those around them. And so it was two years later that they had found a home.

Yo-Mai was around the same age as the Furphy boys, and they called her Yody. Often the boys would play at the main house with her. They enjoyed the strange customs of her parents, but never to the extent of embarrassing her, even when Yody had to unplait her father's hair.

One day after school in the late summer, all three were helping the parents pick corn. The procedure was to move around the outside of the crop, for this was where the corn had ripened. The morning and afternoon sun, combined with the hot northerly winds, had the outer ranks of corn wilting to the point where they were most vulnerable, their inner leaves rolling back to reveal the secret of the corn: a phallic cob studded with columns of fecund golden grains. As the corn was picked the plant was snapped over, allowing the row behind it to ripen for harvest next day.

As usual, Yody and Joe fell behind the others. To reach the corn they both needed to pull on the plant and some-times swing on the stem to bring it to the ground. Yody had tired of the chore and decided to hide from Joe. She moved into the crop, forcing her small body between the stalks, calling to Joe when she felt she had sufficient start, then she stopped to look around. Sitting in the cool, semi-dark forest of corn, she lowered her breathing rate. Joe was close by and heading in her direction. Yody decided to move further into what must have been near the centre of the crop, when sud-denly she burst into a cleared area, about room size and full of light. The clearing was stacked with fresh vegetables: let-tuce, carrots, potatoes and corn cobs with their protruding dark tassels. This was unusual enough for Yody to give up the game and call Joe. He had lost the trail slightly but her continued calls had him veering to the left, until he too stumbled into what looked like a greengrocer's shop without a roof.

Yody had often mentioned to Joe her parents' concern that much of their vegetable and fruit crops seemed to dis-appear just before their harvest. It was a mystery the Chinese couple had often tried to explain to others on the farm, most of whom thought it a ploy to exaggerate what already seemed to them to be abundant harvests.

The children, realising they had all but solved the mystery, did not stop to ponder the reasons but rather obeyed their instincts and followed a lightly used track that led back into the corn in the opposite direction from which they had entered. Five minutes later they worked out where they were, for they could now hear the creek, and soon after they saw light at the edge of the crop, and then they were clear.

That night Ming, Hunter, Samuel and Anderson waited, crouched in the corn in full view of the track that led down to the river. Yody and Joe had excitedly told Ming of their discovery, then led him to the hideout of hidden fruits, the quality and size taking his breath, the pride of seeing the choicest of his crop resting on a clean matting of dried corn leaves slowly giving way to anger on realising that this was the first stage of a planned movement of stolen produce. Anderson, on hearing Ming's story, was equally outraged, not so much from the loss of property as from the stigma associated with the likely culprits.

The moon reflected on the glassy surface of the water. The river at this spot, and a hundred yards on either side, followed a straight course. It slowed, indicating an even but deeper than normal riverbed.

Anderson held the single-barrel gun. An hour earlier he had carefully loaded by hand and rod, packing the wads, gunpowder, lead, then finally the flint. He would have liked to test-fire but decided against it for fear of the noise warning of his intentions. Hunter and Samuel held ropes. Ming appeared to be empty-handed, until his movement allowed the moonlight to reflect on the blade of a well-used vegetable knife under his belt.

Just before midnight a breeze filtered down the valley. The placid water formed small ripples that in turn gave the motionless reflections some life. The trees on the far bank appeared to sway, acknowledging relief from the hot day by releasing leaves and small branches that marked the river's changing surface and for a moment disguised the bark canoes. But when these reached the middle of the river the moon, no longer part hidden by trees on the opposite bank, illuminated the eyes, teeth, and fingernails of three male Aborigines, all in the one canoe, one of them holding the second canoe at arm's length, their dark bodies camouflaged against the inner sides of the boat.

Anderson's plan was to let the thieves disembark and load the stolen cargo before confronting them, thus ensuring sufficient evidence. They had transferred the produce onto large bark slabs, and after three trips had eventually filled the bark canoe. On their last trip Anderson moved out of the corn and beckoned to the others. They quickly realised then that if the Aborigines spotted them they could disperse into the corn and disappear, and so the plan was changed and they moved back into the shelter of the corn, having decided to tackle them as they approached their canoes, an advantage that would have them with their backs to the corn and the robbers nowhere to go but the river.

John and Joe had overheard the plan. Like all important decisions, the discussion took place in Anderson's office attached to the main house, and the boys had listened at the window. Samuel argued that the police should take charge of the apprehension. Anderson and Hunter believed this would take too long. Ming's opinion was not sought. Joe and John moved away from the window for fear of being spotted by Yody or her mother, whose cottage was on the same side of the main house. It was then that John suggested they should watch the chase that night.

The boys took up their position fifty yards downstream. The three Aborigines appeared. Silent in their movement like animals in the night, they made their way to the water's edge. Anderson stepped clear of the corn, gun to his shoulder. The others followed. 'Stop and raise your hands!' Anderson bellowed.

What followed next surprised the four. The Aborigines sank into the river without a splash and disappeared. Their pursuers were at the water's edge now, Anderson furious, his face red with rage and his mind losing control. His large hands tightened around the gun.

They scanned the river, waiting for the inevitable head to appear, not noticing the loaded canoe gently moving away from the bank. When they did see it, it was too much for Anderson, who fired into the water beneath the boat. It was a lucky shot, taking the shoulder of the younger Aborigine, who surfaced, then rolled back and under. The canoe continued, reached the other side. Two blacks clambered up the bank and disappeared into the scrub.

Anderson was satisfied. His only shot had found its mark. That would be sufficient warning. Ming was happy too, for he saw that the canoe with the load of stolen vegetables lay at the bank, easily recoverable.

John and Joe had seen the shooting. It was time to move quickly back to their cottage. John had moved up the bank. Joe had turned to follow when he noticed a movement in the water: the wounded Aborigine kicking, trying to push his body onto the muddy bank but then sliding back, his energy gradually subsiding, his blood on the mud bank like glazed pottery in the moonlight.

Joe hesitated, then moved down the bank and, stretching, reached for the young man's arm and pulled him clear of the water. He removed his shirt and singlet, tying the singlet under the arm and over the gaping wound. He hesitated, wondering if there was more he could or should do. The Aborigine was looking at Joe with big calm eyes that defied the young body as its life ebbed and then faded. Joe waited until death came, then ran back to the cottage, having replaced his shirt on the way.

Nothing was said about the incident that night. Indeed, no one was supposed to know. Samuel was ashamed of the outcome and furious that the others had not heeded his advice to call the police. Joe decided not to tell of his encounter with the dying man. That night, in bed talking over the day's event, Joe was surprised when John remarked that they got what they deserved and that Anderson was a hero. It was then that for the first time Joe realised how different they were.

CHAPTER 4

On The
Move

IN THE EARLY 1860s and after many years at Kangaroo Ground, the Furphy family packed their belongings into two wagons and a cart. All of these had been made by Samuel and John in their spare time at the blacksmith's shop. Trained by Hunter, John had become an excellent wheelwright, and his skill in design was sought by others. Of particular interest to those in the district were horse-drawn buggies built lower to the ground but still retaining a wheel of standard size. This was achieved by forging the axle to drop down between the wheel centres, thereby reducing the centre of gravity.

The idea had come to John after a tragedy struck the family fifteen months earlier. Their sister Jane, just four years old, was rushed back to the farm on her second day at school. She had for some time suffered from a form of whooping cough, but on this day she seemed close to death. She was taken to Anderson's house. Samuel and Judith consulted everyone they could find for an opinion on what was best to do. Hunter and Millie, Yo-Mai and Ming, and

Anderson all agreed that her only chance was to get to Melbourne town, fast.

Anderson harnessed his best horse, a powerful jet-black beast capable of galloping the entire fifteen miles to Melbourne. The traces were connected to his new buggy. He had purchased it, fully imported from America, with the intention of copying its suspension and braking mechanisms. It had been developed for the mid-west plains of America. Flat prairie-type land and long distances were covered quickly by large thin wheels which carried the disproportionately small, lightly sprung carriage.

Jane was tucked tightly into her wooden cradle base and placed beside Samuel. There was little time for farewell and good wishes. Judith was to remember the face of her daughter, the torment of pain mixed with the fear of the unknown trip ahead.

It was the last time they were to see each other. Eleven miles on and within sight of the lights of Melbourne set against a dark sunset, the new buggy flipped on rounding a bend. Propelled by its height, it rolled several times, throwing Samuel clear, but not Jane. Her cradle had caught between the seat and wheel, her small body twisted between the broken hickory spokes and the wheel rim.

Over the next weeks and months the two brothers watched the grief-stricken parents, each trying to console each other. But Samuel would not forgive himself. John, seeing his father's remorse, suggested that the cause of the buggy tipping was its shape and size, citing the unstable penny-farthing bike, so high off the ground and now superseded by the more fashionable and stable two-wheeler, as an example. While not accepting that this was the cause of the accident, Samuel was enthusiastic to work with his son, and soon a new range of buggy shapes appeared on the roads around the area.

It was at about that time that Samuel and Judith contemplated more earnestly their desire to one day be independent of Anderson's farm. The boys were now young men who could earn a man's wage, John as an assistant to a blacksmith, Joe content with the mundane tasks around the farm. But Joe was also a handy striker at the forge. His long thin body and arms somehow concealed hidden muscles. As the big hammer gathered momentum, the higher lift allowed greater speed on the downswing and so his impact on the reddened iron was superior to the swing of the shorter, more nuggety and well-muscled lads considered by others the correct build for that heavy work. All things considered, it was time to make a new life for themselves elsewhere—in the Kyneton region.

Samuel had given his boss sufficient notice of their intention to leave. Anderson, a proud man able to conceal his emotion, yet moved close to Samuel when the moment of parting came. They shook hands, and for some moments held each other with their eyes. The years had brought a mutual respect, until now never expressed.

John and his father, in the larger of the two horse lorries, stacked high with their belongings, led the way down the farm track towards the road. Joe and his mother followed in a smaller cart, but with an equally large load. Those they loved, whom they had depended on all those years, remained clustered where they had said their farewells moments earlier, the trail of dust between them gradually thinning, the earthy particles from the farm that bound them now severed by the morning breeze.

Joe and his mother together looked down at the wicker basket on her lap, loaded with vegetables from Ming and his family, then looked at each other, their eyes welling with tears. John and his father looked straight ahead along the road to change and prosperity.

CHAPTER 5

A Melbourne Stopover

ON THEIR WAY to Kyneton the wagons carrying the Furphys and their belongings had reached the flat plains of the Yarra Valley on the outskirts of Melbourne. Seen from a distance in the late afternoon, plumes of dust from behind the wagons blotched the clear blue sky. By early evening they had arrived at Cleary's Hotel on the banks of the Yarra and in the centre of a bustling city. Samuel and Judith noticed that the tents had given way to substantial buildings, fine timber dwellings, brick shops and warehouses, some with ornate iron around doors and windows. Some shops had a lean-to reaching out to the road proper, allowing a clear walkway beneath, different from the shops in Ireland whose frontage was bold and square—two windows, a door, and the only attachment a sign that swung above the door. They had heard from Anderson that the lean-to was referred to as a 'verandah' and that the idea was similar to the American boardwalk without the raised walkway.

John and Joe had led the horses to the rear of the hotel.

They were surprised at the number of horses housed, and had to separate the four horses into pairs to obtain a tethering position. The sound of their hoofs on the bluestone flooring did not seem to disturb the other horses; indeed even their beasts remained placid in the new surrounds. Exhausted by the journey and relieved of their harness, they stood uninterested and relaxed.

The family had one day to see Melbourne before setting off for Kyneton. That evening, in the hotel's plush dining room, they made plans. Each had different ideas on what they should see. Samuel insisted they should go to the wharves and show the boys the pier where nineteen years earlier they had landed in Australia. John agreed, excited at the thought of a chance look at the steam vessels and their cargo. Judith was wanting to buy dress material and visit the library, and Joe wanted to visit the new Royal Botanic Gardens. In the end it was decided that if they started early enough it would be possible to accommodate all suggestions.

The early morning sun reached through the small windows of the dining room, lighting the far wall with a subdued glow as Samuel and Judith came down for breakfast with their boys. The tables, laden with silver utensils and cutlery, were unoccupied except for another family seated in the far corner, abuzz with muted excitement. As the room filled, the mood of happy anticipation caught up the guests and the room seemed brighter, warmer. The Furphys sat among them, eagerly discussing what the day might hold.

It was only a half-mile downstream from the hotel that they noticed jetties reaching into the waterway, their function to hold an assortment of sailing craft in some form of order. Varying sizes of ship, all ocean-going, seemed to rest in the calm waters of the river, their sails unevenly rolled around outreaching masts. On decks and jetties a flurry of activity prevailed as cargo was hauled to waiting lorries. A little further along was a larger pier familiar to Samuel and Judith. Even though alterations and additions had changed this landing place, they were able to find the very spot where nineteen years earlier they had stepped from the gangplank. And then they held each other. 'As strong as the ropes that hold these ships, I love you,' Samuel whispered in her ear. Joe, sensing their happiness, went to them, and the three embraced. John was inspecting cargo recently unloaded, machinery and implements from America and England.

Samuel, seeing how Joe shared their moment of reminiscence, wondered at the nature of this boy, so different from others: unaggressive, a container of hoarded moments that mellowed his youth. Catching his eye, Samuel winked at his son, gripped him by the shoulder. 'Let's go, time to buy your mother a present.'

A hundred yards in from the river confines, substantial buildings housing new industry were interspersed with fashionable shops. Here a calm confidence prevailed, a less exuberant trading indicating the centre of a future city. Judith was enjoying herself, stopping, exploring side streets, peering into windows. She disappeared into one of the larger stores. One hour later she emerged, clad in a new outfit. Poised and excited, she joined the others, her heart racing with happiness.

Madame Rennie's coffee palace was well known for its quality foods and beverages. The four sat at a window table, secure and rested from the noise and bustle of the street beyond. At the front of the establishment was a large metal coffee grinder the size of a man, bright red in colour, with two huge flywheels on either side which were kept turning by four youths who took it in turns. Another youth working from a higher platform fed the machine beans, a dipperful at a time, and on street level two pretty girls bagged the ground coffee and sold it to passing traffic.

John suggested to his father that the wheels could be turned by a small steam-driven engine, thus eliminating the need for labour by more than half. Samuel and Judith, ever proud of their son's enterprise, hastily agreed. All three were dampened when Joe suggested that those eating and drinking there might be offended by the noise, smoke and steam. John, annoyed at this sign of social concern in his brother, quickly countered by explaining that of course the engine would be enclosed in an engine room.

That seemed to put an end to the subject, and it was not long before they were reminiscing about the day's events, Joe reminding them more than once of the one remaining destination.

And so in the late afternoon they crossed Princes Bridge. Beneath raced the swirling waters of the Yarra River, swollen by the heavy spring rains that had fallen on the mountains to the east. The road to South Melbourne resembled a boulevard, a rich artery, wide and straight, with the driveways of wealthy mansions as its capillaries. Over the bridge they turned to the left, following the river upstream for a half-mile. Here the flat terrain gave way to undulating hills, small valleys with billabongs and creeks that meandered to the river, in all two square miles of public land proclaimed and identified as a botanical site by Charles La Trobe.

The perimeter of the gardens was now well established, within it a vast number of plant species from all over the world. These had been gathered with great energy by Baron Ferdinand von Mueller, and planted in their formal botanical settings, each with grave-like identification neatly staked at their base. Elsewhere landscaping on a major scale was taking place: hundreds of men and many horses laboured, shifting soil, altering watercourses and creating several large lakes.

Overlooking the activity, the Furphys sat, shaded from

the late afternoon sun. Now weary from their day of walking, they relaxed. Samuel had his boots off, John seemed bored, Joe had wandered down a path admiring a variety of roses (an interest that stayed with him for a lifetime).

It was here that he overheard two men arguing. They were on an adjacent path and hidden by shrubbery. Joe moved to a position where he could now see plainly, and to his great surprise recognised both men. They had stayed at Cleary's Hotel the night before and Joe had noticed the names on their luggage: Baron Ferdinand von Mueller and William Guilfoyle. Guilfoyle had recently taken over from von Mueller the management and planning of the site. His less formal approach to landscaping required the re-establishing of many plant species. Von Mueller was obviously not convinced that his layout of the garden should be rearranged.

That night Joe recorded what he could remember of the conversation between the two. The arguments for and against were given along with a view of his own, slightly favouring the plans of Guilfoyle. Before he knew it he had compiled an interesting essay, a layman's opinion, and he thought even then of seeking its publication.

CHAPTER 6

Kyneton and Leonie

TWENTY MILES north-west of Melbourne the travellers noticed a change in the countryside. The flat grasslands gave way to hills and valleys, here and there clusters of human endeavour, protected by the swelling hills; there was digging, sifting, panning with the urgency of an infant gulping at the nipple—people with a hunger for gold.

There were others on the road, some in lighter drays and gigs that passed them. All seemed determined, as if their particular destination was all that mattered. Like many others who took that north-west road out of Melbourne in those heady days, a sense of excitement showed on their faces: travellers from all countries of the world, rich and poor, their mode of transport a variety of human and animal energy.

On the second day, and roughly halfway to Kyneton, they approached the notorious Black Forest, an area that could not be avoided: steep hills lay on one side and sheer cliffs on the other, a lock to the treasure chest of gold country that lay beyond; the only key was the determination of each man and woman to get through. A canopy of dense eucalypts darkened the forest floor and the road became a series of tracks veering left and right, chasing firmer ground. Samuel drove the larger of the wagons, Joe had the reins of the other, and John was running ahead checking for fresh tracks.

They had made good progress until they were stopped by others ahead who had become bogged. Two family groups were all pushing and pulling their wagons. Now there were five vehicles and Samuel decided it was time for a conference. The menfolk talked, then inspected the ground on a ridge to the right, high ground but impossible to pass because of several large trees.

Joe and John were handy with an axe, and in a short time they had a track cleared, much to the admiration of a mother and her two daughters. The mother had been driving one of their two wagons, her husband the other, and now because they were the first in line they steered their wagons to the newly cleared track. The gradient was steep and John noticed the anxiety on the women's faces, particularly one they called Sarah. He moved over to them, taking the lead horse at short rein, and led them along the sloping track until they were back on level ground.

Soon the group emerged from the forest and set up camp. That night they shared supper, secure in their numbers from another danger that preyed on stranded or resting travellers in the vicinity of the forest—the bushranger. Through a gentle swirl of smoke John and Sarah exchanged glances.

Kyneton in the 1860s was more established than the surrounding towns of Castlemaine, Talbot and Coldstream. It was the centre for commerce and government facilities struggling to keep pace with the itinerant population. The immediate farming district was an important source of food for hungry miners and exhausted animals.

Samuel rented a cottage on the edge of town in those

first weeks. After five weeks he had decided to purchase closer to town on Main Street, next to the Cobb & Co. passenger terminal. The price was low by comparison. Samuel knew that others had not made an offer for it because of the continual movement, the coming and going of passengers at all hours, day and night. This inconvenience could be tolerated if the site became valuable after some time, which he thought it might.

John was successful in applying to the local blacksmiths Hanks & Lindseys for an apprenticeship. Samuel leased a steam engine and with Joe they moved around the farms hitching the machine to various farm implements owned by wealthy pastoralists who had been able to increase their holdings as out-of-luck miners moved on. Judith was helping out at the government school and for two days a week was paid to teach English to the children of miners, whose continual relocation hampered the children's studies.

And so for the next year or so it seemed that the family was able to consolidate. There was enough money for them to live comfortably. Samuel, who had become increasingly involved in the local branch of the Temperance Society, was considered by some to be a leader of the upright bunch. Indeed, more than once they had encouraged him to represent them on the local council. He had confided in John that had it not been for the late night drinking after every meeting, he might have considered nominating. These matters were never discussed with Joe, for Samuel knew of Joe's views on the Society—'pious dubbly dumd' he called them.

While Samuel and John grew closer, Joe was becoming more and more independent of the family. He was not a great mixer, being more reclusive, his sympathies increasingly attuned to the miners and their socialist comradeship, their frank and casual character. His few friends of a more imaginative cast of mind were those he met regularly at the local Mechanics' Institute and who wrote about what they saw as the real journeys of life: the hardship and the kindness, the colour and sincerity of ordinary folk—the Tom Collinses of the world.

It was about this time that John announced his intention to marry Sarah Vaughan. Her family too had settled in Kyneton, and since they had met that day in the Black Forest a firm though not intimate friendship had grown between the two families. A similar relationship with John and Sarah blossomed, but as two flowers growing through a drought, rigid and sparse, unable to bloom in the fullness of ripe touch. Sarah was broad of hip. A wide face and strong jaw tried to dominate her facial expression but managed only to accentuate her rather bland look.

The marriage ceremony held in the Masonic hall was like any other meeting of the Temperance Society—but worse, Joe thought: the formal costume and polite gestures made John and Sarah seem phoney, remote, masking anything that might have made them real. But when John rose to salute his bride and thank his guests Joe found himself admiring his eloquence and his relaxed sincerity. In contrast to his own frequent shyness in public, he saw how clever his brother was at speaking in public.

In the next year Samuel embarked on a new business venture, as a seed and produce merchant. He rented a warehouse, dealing directly with the farmers with whom he had worked.

Joe drifted into many jobs, having decided to abandon the steam driving after a nasty incident that very nearly had him in gaol. One hot and dry afternoon towards the end of the day, a fire started in stubble thirty yards downwind from where the engine operated on a property owned by one Richard Wiltshire. By the time Joe had noticed the smoke, the fire had taken hold. It roared through the sixty-acre paddock of stubble, taking some outbuildings but sparing the main house. Eventually it burnt itself out on the edge of a forest.

Wiltshire, a big man, now exhausted by the fire-fighting, approached Joe, who also had helped save the main barn. Exhausted too but now with the added burden of blame, Joe braced himself as the large reddened face of Wiltshire only inches away dominated the immediate air space. Specks of black ash lay like dead confetti on the bridge of his nose and forehead. He insisted that they inspect the steam engine as soon as the local constabulary arrived.

As they approached the huge machine Joe saw it as a monster, indeed alive and stamping its feet, stark on the blackened soil with puffs of smoke still rising from burnt piles of thrashed husks and stalks. The reality of it came back into focus as they inspected the chimney stack: rust had eaten a pattern of holes through the metal below the area of the spark arrester. Wiltshire was pointing to it with one hand and inviting the constable to climb up for closer inspection with the other. The rusted section was lifted away from the base. It would be taken as evidence if charges were laid.

When Joe arrived home he was not surprised that the family already knew of the fire at Wiltshire's. Strange that news of disasters spread an abandon of light gossip, while news of a find on the fields was shrouded, rumoured, delayed, as if news of potential wealth were despised by those who missed out.

Samuel had realised immediately what had probably happened. He felt guilty, knowing that the engine had started other small fires that he and Joe had been able to control. They had talked of repairing the rusted chimney, but his new business had consumed his time.

Samuel and Joe talked long into the night and a plan

was devised that might stop Wiltshire from laying charges. The steam engine was valuable equipment and in working order worth at least £400. The next day Samuel and his son called on Wiltshire. Apologising, they offered the machine as reimbursement for damage done. Wiltshire considered for some time then agreed to accept the offer and take the matter no further.

Joe drifted into many jobs, wood-cutting, farm labouring and bullock-driving. The last was his favourite work, especially driving for Hennessy. Hennessy had several teams carting grain and wool from Echuca to Melbourne via Kyneton, and Joe quickly became the changeover driver for the Kyneton–Melbourne run. Return trips carried cargo of a more domestic type: kerosene, cloth and hardware, nails, wire and liquor.

On these more frequent trips to Melbourne Joe would hand-deliver letters, poems and occasionally short stories to the *Bulletin* and the *Argus*, works compiled by the group of amateur writers who worked late into the night at the Mechanics' Institute in Kyneton. On his return he would bring books and manuscripts borrowed from the State Library, all of which were eagerly read by a devout and somewhat deprived group who saw their Institute as others would see their church.

On one such trip home Joe was overtaken by a wild storm and with the Black Forest area ahead he decided to stay overnight at the Vineyard Hotel on the Daylesford–Glenlyon road. He had heard both good and bad stories of Zelie the Frenchwoman and her hotel.

A paddock at the rear of the hotel seemed a convenient place to tether the bullocks, but first he would need to ask permission. Unable to leave the team, he beckoned to a youth to stand by his lead bullock, while he asked at the hotel. The youth, dressed in a large coat and beret, obliged, and Joe noticed the confident stance of this lightly built teenager.

Inside the front door there was a short passage with doors on either side that opened into small bars, and at the end a door with a notice saying 'Guests'. Joe entered and there was Zelie. Joe recalled stories of her sometimes over-exuberant welcome and was surprised, when introducing himself how shy and nervous he was of this woman and her doubtful reputation. She had been most obliging about his bullocks and as well was suggesting he should take a hot bath before dinner, even offering to cart some hot water from the copper at the rear of the hotel to the bathroom. 'A bath would be lovely, but allow me to at least carry my bath water.' Joe thanked her somewhat protectively. 'All right, dinner at eight.' She handed him the keys to room number four.

Joe returned to the team. Thanking the youth, he offered a coin, noticing the fine, slender hand and then the delicate features around the nose and eyes, not the hands and face of an Irish youth, more gypsy-like. Then as he turned he noticed plaited hair falling down her back from under the beret.

Joe carried a bucket of hot water in each hand from a small room set off the verandah to the rear passage of the hotel that would lead to the bathroom. It required that he pass what could only be the kitchen as the smells of pork and sweet potatoes wafted into the passage.

Glancing in, he noticed the cook, who at first he thought was Zelie, but then saw it was someone much younger, a lot younger, the sharp, hardened features of her mother blunted with the rounded warmth of youth. Her brown eyes turned to meet this intruder. The fright gave way to a nervous smile—they had met earlier.

Joe remembered that meal and who served it to him on

that cold winter's night. The hotel became a stopover on his more frequent trips, and when he wasn't driving bullocks he found work in the area anyway. Leonie and her mother Zelie extended welcome—Zelie's more a slap on the back, Leonie's the gentle touch of love.

CHAPTER 7

Morals, Enterprise and Socialism

LATER IN LIFE Joe often thought of those early days in Kyneton. The promise of his years of bullock-driving had petered out, and now he worked as a mere hand in his brother's foundry in Shepparton. But those journeys in the outback had given him the material for what had now become his real life: his writing.

On the night before he was to take John's grain-stripper to Melbourne, he had packed his bags in readiness for the early start in the morning. The stripper was ready loaded. Before sleeping he walked through the moonlight in his backyard to the bank of the Goulburn River. The moon, a vivid reflection on the water, reminded him of the shooting of the Aboriginal youth on the moonlit waters of the Yarra at Kangaroo Ground. The memory had often returned to him with a sense of guilt, and he wondered about the spirits, and about the power of Aboriginal mythology.

He turned his thoughts to the moon he remembered around Kyneton, the nights with Leonie, in the fields, on the back roads and through the window of room number four at Zelie's hotel. It had been a beacon that guided them through tough times, and now that same moon seemed to mock their eroded dreams. As the years went by the excitement and significance of those early days with each other had become a blank.

Leonie and her sons seemed uninterested in his trip the next day. They were used to the long trips away when for weeks and months he went bullock-driving on the northern plains. Then the solitude of the open plains was an escape from the monotony of foundry work and his increasingly self-righteous brother, a chance to provide without the dependence on the foundry pay packet. Best of all were the characters, the friendships, the yarns to be told.

He had packed as he would for his journeys north, but with some additions, a suit and matching overcoat made in England and purchased, or, more accurately, acquired, from a traveller after a late night two-up game in Echuca. Joe would always hasten to explain that it was not a case of literally winning the clothes off the unlucky gambler's back, but that the traveller sold fine clothing to the gentry of the area and when light on cash sometimes gambled his stock. It fitted well and accentuated his tall, lean build. And in Melbourne he would be meeting Kate Baker, his friend and admirer, a teacher of literature who now lived in Melbourne but had once taught in a tiny school in northern Victoria. She was helping him with *Such Is Life*, which had to be shortened in some way if it was to have a chance of publication.

Early the next morning Joe and his sons Felix and Sam walked to the foundry. The boys now were both working most days at their uncle's foundry. Joe was secretly disappointed that they had not been more venturesome and ambitious in their vocations, but as Leonie had often reminded him, his absence from the family had hindered the boys' progress, and he had to admit that it might well have been the case.

The paddock alongside the foundry had a small area fenced off, and already men had gathered to farewell the grain-stripper, now set atop a wagon and tied down with heavy flaxen ropes. It did indeed look splendid in the early morning sun, the bright red woodwork framing dull silver metal sheet, with cast cogs and other heavy iron components painted in a glossy black and across both sides fine signwriting in scrolls that matched the delicate curves of forged handrails and levers.

John was moving around the machine like a judge moving around an exhibit in order to calculate points. Completely satisfied, he stopped and checked his watch, the heavy silver chain spilling from his pocket as he brought it into focus. Seven o'clock and they were due to leave. Just in time, Joe led the team of bullocks, eight in all and harnessed in pairs, to the front of the lorry. A final instruction from John and then, with a long but gentle 'Ya'aaa' from Joe, the team strained on the traces. There was a cheer from several of the workers as the team and its cargo moved out onto the street bound for Seymour and then Melbourne by rail.

Once on the open road, Joe and Dan, one of this brother's foundry workers, would take it in turns to walk with the lead bullocks, and so when not walking, the other man could rest by riding on the wagon. Joe had chosen Dan as his assistant on the journey, not for his experience as this was nonexistent, but because of his slow and somewhat gentle disposition, a prerequisite for successful bullock-driving.

When they were clear of the town and making good progress Joe was relieved by Dan and climbed aboard, making himself comfortable on the back of the wagon. Sitting on some padded hessian and leaning against their suitcases, his mind went back to other teams he had driven over the years.

It had started in Kyneton around the time he met

Leonie, and he had been driving off and on ever since. Joe and Leonie were married in Kyneton, a small wedding with Zelie and three or four of her men friends on one side of the church and Joe's family plus a few of his mates from the Mechanics' Institute on the other. In that same year his parents sold a prosperous business and moved to a land settlement scheme in the Colbinabbin–Rushworth area. Zelie sold her hotel and moved to the brighter lights of Melbourne. Her daughter off her hands, she became an even more risqué tutor of sorts to the young men of that virgin city.

Joe battled from one job to another. Work on the goldfields was scarce and running out, people were moving out to other fields in the east of the colony, and Joe found himself doing what he enjoyed most, driving bullocks, which also took him further afield. The towns along the Murray River to the north were now the feeder towns for the transport of goods, particularly rural produce. Joe would take Leonie on these long trips, sometimes for weeks on end, until she became pregnant. That was when they started to become independent of each other, Leonie seemingly content to live her own life.

They had left Kyneton to follow his parents. Joe rented a small cottage located at the northern end of Samuel and Judith's farm. Leonie was secure here with her newborn son, though she had a rather distant relationship with her in-laws, who had never warmed to her but for Joe's sake cared for her at least while he was away. The little village of Wanalta Creek was two miles down the road and Leonie would often walk with the baby to do her shopping, at the same time selling embroidered cloth that would be made into tablecloths, pillows and sheets by local farmers' wives.

Joe was closer to the Murray River and it was not long before he had secured regular deliveries between Rochester and Echuca with his own team of bullocks. It was through the winter months that work became scarce, and rather than sell his team he moved north of the Murray into central New South Wales, carting wool that would be shipped down the Darling to the ports on the Murray, the swollen rivers in winter and early spring the only chance for delivery from the thousands of miles of new land that had no roads.

These trips kept him away for up to four months at a time, but the financial rewards were good, and now that he owned his team he could choose his clients, so that like the shearing teams he could return each season. The sheep farms around Hay and Balranald were large holdings, so sparse and barren that they required huge tracts of land to feed an average-sized flock of around two thousand head.

In the shearing season other drivers and their teams arrived to cope with the transportation, and along with an influx of shearers and rouseabouts the inland came alive in a meandering fashion, slow as old man river, a contrast to the helter-skelter of the goldfields. It was on these occasions that Joe found true companionship with characters who were suited to the bush but not the city, who around a camp fire could espouse their own idiosyncratic philosophies about their fellow man.

Joe was jolted from his reverie by the screech of cockatoos and realised it was time to move down off the wagon and make his way to the front of the team. Dan was pleased at the break. His arms were tired from the constant pulling of the lead bullock, who tended to veer to the left for no apparent reason. He pointed this out to Joe, who without hesitation adjusted a leather strap around the collar by two notches. The collar straightened itself and within the next ten yards the animal seemed more comfortable. The muscles in its neck loosened as it lifted its head to the way ahead.

At Murchison they followed the Goulburn River south to Nagambie, camping overnight at those locations. On the fourth day they reached Seymour at around midday. They would need the afternoon to load the grain-stripper onto a flat-deck rail car.

By midday the following day all the rail trucks were loaded. The steam engine alone on the tracks seemed like a grotesque hissing monster until it backed up and joined a line of loaded trucks, complete with the guard's van at the rear.

Joe had got permission to ride in the guard's van. Dan was to wait a few days in the hope that a load might need transporting north from the Seymour railyards. If not he was to return home with the bullocks and wagon.

As the train moved slowly away, pulled by a chugging giant that breathed blotches of black smoke while seemingly floating on a mist of pure white steam, Joe could not help admiring its capacity to pull.

The guard's name was Henry Whelan. He had introduced himself earlier, and now that the train had settled at its regular speed he lit up a small kerosene burner and boiled a billy—it would be a six-hour trip to Melbourne, ample time to eat damper that he had made back in Seymour, sip some tea and have a yarn.

They talked of the recent fighting at Ballarat, the miners marching in the streets, protesting against the fees and taxes. It was big news in Melbourne, and Henry had some up-to-date news on the events which by now were a cause for concern for the gentry of the port city who relied on the gold wealth for their increasing ambitions.

Bottom Swage

CHAPTER 8

Train-jumpers

WORD OF TENSION on the gold-
fields around Ballarat had spread to other fields. Mines were
yielding less as the easy gold close to the surface was scav-
enged by a relentless mass of human muscle. Individuals
with pick and shovel were being pushed aside by companies
which seemed able to pay the increased fees that were needed to take out even the smallest leases.

Thirty odd years before the stockade at Eureka had been
the scene of bloody fighting between miners and police. A
number were killed before a truce was called. Henry
Whelan's wife's brother was one of those killed, and he
would have been too if his wife had not persuaded him to
quit the mines and join the railways. It turned out all right
though. Henry was sifting the tea through his teeth then
chewing on the damper. "Cause they formed some sort of
workman's union, and that's been an example to all of us.'
Joe nodded.

The train had slowed now as it began its long haul to
the top of a mountain range. 'I'm expecting we'll have some

extra passengers shortly. Better be ready to help pull 'em aboard.' Henry gave Joe a look of daring comradeship. He had moved to the door and was leaning out, looking ahead. He signalled to Joe to do likewise on the other side. Joe noticed that the train had slowed almost to a walking pace. His eyes, momentarily blinded by smoke and soot, narrowed to peer ahead as he leant out his side.

Then he saw, clambering up the bank, a family—the father with the youngest in his arms, the other two children running and reaching for their mother's skirts. The guard's van was passing them now but they were making ground. The father was the first to reach the doorway. He hesitated, looking back. Passing the small child into Joe's arms, he waited seconds until the mother and other children were beside him. Then, gathering the younger of the two with one arm, he took his wife's hand with the other. They had lost ground and were now running fast to draw level with the van. Joe was reaching out, and as they drew level he took the second child. The mother soon had a firm grip on the door rail, her other hand reaching back to take hold of the remaining child, but she could not reach.

Joe pulled her aboard as the father got hold of the child, but he was behind again now and the train seemed to be gathering speed as it levelled at the top of a ridge. He was a strong man and again he drew level, but Joe could see he would not keep up for long. Joe was lying on the floor, his shoulders well clear of the doorway. He had hold of the father and now as he pulled him closer he felt his body slipping. He was about to let go when he felt the firm support of Henry's clasp on his ankles. Now anchored, he held tight as the child was passed up to the mother, and then the father was aboard.

Henry soon had more water on the boil for tea and there was some damper left over that would be shared around. Joe knew that Henry was risking his job. There were posters on all stations warning against train-jumping, and heaven knows what penalties were imposed on those caught, or what they'd do if an employee was found to be assisting them—at the very least he'd lose his job, and there was a chance he'd go to gaol.

'Will they be checking for tickets at the station?' the father of the young family asked.

Henry considered the question. Most of the jumpers had been single fellows and they usually abandoned the train well out from the platform. The train was slowing now and Henry knew the station was not far away.

'I'll tell you what now, when the train stops you should leave through that door. It'll be the opposite to the platform side. Then make your way across the tracks and hide under some stationary rolling trucks until dark. When it's dark you should be able to find your way out to the road.'

Only Mary showed signs of anxiety, the children accepting the plan as routine. Glancing out, Joe noticed a build-up of cottages, small rows interspersed with warehouses and factories, cobblestone roads with a movement of people and animals on its hard surface. The steam whistle from this rolling monster as it crossed a main road portrayed a moment of fixed heads, people turned in admiration, wide-eyed, the horses with heads back, eyes gleaming black and frightened.

The train was stopping. Henry looked out, checking which side was the platform, then pointed to the side they should make their exit. A sudden jolt, then silence before a hiss of steam announced the end of the journey.

Joe had decided that he would help them escape the confines of the railyard. He had asked Henry about the safe-keeping of the train's cargo. Tomorrow being Sunday meant that the stripper would remain loaded until Monday morning. 'Not the sort of stripper I'd be after anyways. I reckons she'll be safe,' he said with a slow grin.

Joe had some time to spare before he need walk the short distance upriver to Richmond and Kate's house, and he knew of a lodging house that owed him a favour nearby. Better they be off the streets with the young 'uns anyway, he thought.

'I'll be with youse for a while,' Joe muttered as he lowered his long frame to the ground.

'Good luck,' Henry waved.

'He's a man of gold, that 'un,' Jack, the father, whispered as he gathered the family. 'Follow Joe now, and keep your heads low.'

They had rounded the engine of a stationary train and moved halfway up its length, shadowed by its bulk from the gaslights, which spotlighted only small areas of the yard. The street and safety were no more than two hundred yards away, but in between there was a signal box elevated and manned. From each side a wire mesh fence extended into the darkness. A gate at the edge of the signal box was ajar. It was their only way out. The surrounds of the box were well lit. They sat while Joe and Jack devised a plan.

'Here's what we'll do,' Jack said to Mary. 'One of us'll go over and make ourselves seen, pretend to be injured. When that signal bloke comes down, one of us'll just have to give him an injury too, so you and the kids be ready to run when we call, right through that gate and out to the street.'

'Now who's the injured one?' Joe asked, not too keen on being the assailant. 'Perhaps as I'm older I should be. Besides, I've never hit anyone in my life.'

'OK.' Jack obviously fancied himself as a fighter.

'But don't hit him hard. I'd not want to be up on some serious charge. Perhaps you could just hold him firm like till we all get clear,' Joe tried to explain.

Joe wandered out into the clear and when in sight of the

signalman he fell to the ground. Holding his leg, he began writhing around. It seemed to take some time before he was noticed. In fact Joe was beginning to wonder whether this chap was the right one to be reading signals when he was spotted. A large round face eased itself through a small cubbyhole window, then the man called out, 'You'll have to move, you're on a rail line.'

'I can't,' Joe groaned. 'I thinks me leg's broken.'

'Hang on then.' And soon Joe heard him descending the stairway. 'I'll have to get you off the tracks. There's a train due.' He was breathing heavily, Joe noticed. Jack came in from behind. He had a raised piece of timber, and as he brought it down in line with his rescuer's head Joe rolled him away and the timber splintered on the rail line. 'Hold it back, this fella's a good 'un. I think I can explain.' And as he explained to the bewildered fellow that Jack had just beaten off three others who had broken his leg, Joe saw Mary and the children vanish through the gate.

'It may not be broken,' Jack exclaimed as he lifted Joe. 'Yeah, we'll be right,' Joe agreed, and leaning on Jack they hobbled off, leaving the signalman scratching his lucky head.

They found each other in the adjacent street. 'Follow me,' Joe said as he led the way to Zelie's rooms at the Dragon Hotel. 'I haven't time to take you in,' Joe explained. 'Just go in and ask for Zel. Tell her I sent you and ask if she can put you up for the night. Tomorrow look for work, and good luck.'

Joe felt he had done all he could. He turned and set off up the street towards Richmond two miles to the east.

CHAPTER 9

Different Sundays

KATE BAKER LIVED with her parents in a modest cottage in a factory area now known as Richmond.

On a Sunday morning the Bakers went to church like most others in their street. Kate was excused on this Sunday as Joe was in the house and, as she explained to her parents, he had been on a long journey and would be in need of a good breakfast. As her parents clipped the front gate shut and headed in the direction of the church bells, Kate opened the door of Joe's room and went in.

She put down the tray of food she was carrying, went over to the window and pulled the curtains. On the table were the folds of manuscripts, Joe's writings that she would carefully type for him the next day ready for submission to the *Bulletin*. Together, the night before, they had read Joe's work. Kate was so absorbed in the scenes he had created that an excitement went through her. Through the night she had woken, often the words tumbling into sentences, gathering a momentum that formed a cloak of dark clouds, not threatening but moist, the cloak closing on her, pressing, until she woke in orgasm.

Kate was now in her late twenties, having taught in country schools with a deep dedication that invariably turned into a lingering frustration, as children with potential for further study and professional careers drifted away with parents on the gold trail, or worked the farms in the area from the age of thirteen. The adults in country towns were interested only in their business, their crops and the weather. A number of bachelors who showed a mild interest in her trim but robust figure lost interest quickly when her ability to test their minds mocked a sensuality as vain as country roosters.

The long evenings in between her teaching days were therefore lonely except when Joe's arrival was imminent. He always tried to make Rochester in the early evening with his bullock team *en route* to Echuca, and towards the end of her teaching assignment at Rochester the considerable diversion from the direct route Colbinabbin to Echuca was costing Joe and his bullocks much time and effort as he increased his freight loads to the area, thus forsaking the more lucrative runs north of the Murray River.

They had met at Colbinabbin when she arrived as the first teacher at Wanalta Public School, the same school that would soon be enrolling his boys. On that evening the Furphy clan invited her to supper and Joe was asked to escort her home, a distance of five miles to her schoolhouse quarters. Samuel and Judith, sensing how well Joe and Kate enjoyed mutual discussion on various subjects, had been concerned at the rather anxious look on Leonie's face. Joe had noticed it too and was quick to counter the offer, suggesting that she stay overnight here at his parents' place and that come morning he would gladly escort her back to her residence. Joe relaxed in the realisation that he had not only reassured Leonie but that he and Kate could continue their rather academic philosophising into the night. And so a mutual bond grew, nourished by an intense interest in their ability to ponder the subtle depths of literature.

After eight years in the country Kate moved back to Melbourne. She taught for several more years and enjoyed the students' more sophisticated appreciation of her efforts before taking up her current career as an assistant to the librarian at the Melbourne Library. She wrote regularly to Joe, keeping him informed of the latest acquisitions. Joe in turn would send copies of his work, some of which she hawked to the various news publications.

Her concern to have Joe's work in print became a delightful obsession. Kate interest in the rest of the literary world faded, though she could still show a professional concern to the patrons of the library. There were many men that enjoyed being physically close to her as she perused their reading material in search of some reference or other, or leant forward to identify the selected book title in order to record a gentleman's borrowings. But if they showed a prurient interest she ignored it, preserving always a strictly subdued professional manner towards them.

On this Sunday morning there was little sign of such demeanour. Her clothes were relaxed; her hair, loosed from the tight bun she wore at the library, moved round her shoulders in a dark wave. She went and sat on his bed, watching him until he woke. The green seaweed of her eyes now met the ocean blue of his, a mist on rolling waves, light on a penetrating depth. He held out his arms to her.

On that same Sunday morning, and at precisely that time in northern Victoria, John could see the tiny gathering ahead. As usual the congregation waited outside the small church under the shade of two large peppercorn trees. His horse was tiring from the nine-mile run to the Pine Lodge

Methodists, but it too sensed their distant presence, lifting its head and gathering speed, as John straightened in the saddle so that he would arrive with an authoritative decisiveness that would match his sermon.

At precisely eleven o'clock the doors of the church were opened and the congregation moved to the entrance, but not through it. They fanned out, creating a human funnel through which John strode with a possessed confidence, his mind now rid of any humility and filled with righteousness and power, a condition required to hold them spellbound with his eloquence and to punch home with powerful gestures their obligation to stay on the straight and narrow path.

His brother Joe was at that same moment lying in Kate's arms, his body spent, his normal preoccupation of mind entirely absent in surrender to the moment. It was not a chance encounter, but one premeditated from the very first moments of his arrival at Richmond. The distance between Shepparton and Melbourne, and the impossibility of communicating except by the slow mails, drove a wedge between his country life and the city experiences, and now that Kate was in Melbourne he vowed that then and only then could they satisfy their hunger for one another.

John had selected 'Jobs' as his sermon for today. He had a list of shorthand sermon names that seemed simple and uninspiring: 'Death', 'Treasure', 'Harvest' and so on gave quick and easy reference to the theme, humble words of God that hid the preacher's homely commonsense and the occasional tirade of superlatives. Like all his sermons, 'Jobs' started with 'I remember on one occasion', and then recited an experience as a lead-up to his message. This gave him opportunity to convey his worldly experiences and sometimes his more successful achievements.

The message was one that all could relate to: the old and

young who had their jobs and chores, their lives bound to the rigours of toil. The sermon moved to a higher plane, emphasising jobs that would remain jobs unless there was a striving for excellence. 'The most mundane of jobs can shine before God with effort, clear thinking and a respect for the laws of God, God-fearing habits that clear the mind. Look at the drunkard, his mind befuddled and as a consequence, his job like working in hell.' As the words filled the small church, his flock were all on his side. Few of them had ever touched a drop, but they knew of others that did and that was a source of satisfaction.

The sermon finished with an example of what he considered God's work on earth: 'In Melbourne there is a local exhibit waiting to be judged at the Centennial Show. It is a new type of grain-stripper. It was built by a dedicated band of employees, all of whom to the best of my knowledge are abstainers from alcohol and men of good principle, their minds accordingly disciplined, their bodies pure and strong. Their workmanship has produced an implement that will strip the golden crops to produce food for the hungry. Please God, they will be rewarded for their efforts.'

Many of the congregation would know of the preacher's invention. Those that didn't might enquire at afternoon tea after the service, providing an opportunity for him in a more appropriate civic atmosphere to boast a little of his foundry establishment.

The service closed with the hymn 'On pastures green O God to thee'. John closed the Bible with a military clip that emphasised the rigid discipline of his service and moved back through the doors to the sunlight outside, followed by a humbled flock who were more than sure they were all enlightened.

In Melbourne, Joe and Kate sat happily together in a small courtyard at the side of the house. The folder with

Joe's manuscript was open before them. The work was titled 'The Mythical Sundowner', a series of short stories depicting the pecking order of the bushman, from the squatter and pastoralist to the swagman and sundowner. Mythical in the sense that each seemed born to his lot, and yet all yearned for the other's path. The manuscript was handwritten. Kate had improved on some spelling and suggested an omission or inclusion here and there.

Her mother had prepared the traditional Sunday roast dinner; its warm smells wound through the house and out into the courtyard. Kate sat in delicious suspension between the reverberation of their lovemaking and the Sunday peace of her parents' house. Joe could feel a mixed reaction to his presence—delight that Kate was so happy and relaxed with this man around, and yet concern that he was old enough to be her father. But then he did have this connection with the *Bulletin*, a paper her parents read regularly. They enjoyed the verse and short stories of Banjo Paterson and Henry Lawson but could never quite understand the more infrequent ramblings of Joe Furphy's offerings. Perhaps they thought that was the reason he wrote under the pseudonym 'Warrigal Jack'.

In the afternoon Kate typed the corrected manuscript. Joe walked to the Botanic Gardens where the Sunday spruikers congregated. Their soapbox ritual reminded him of his bush comrades. He loved the refreshing frankness of these urban swagmen, their vocabulary identifying most as having had a stint up country.

The next morning Joe and Kate walked briskly in the chill air to a tram stop at the end of the street. While waiting they were able to flick through the final copy of the 'Mythical Sundowner'. Kate had edged each page with a gold line, and the leather cover also had matching lines, with each corner a display of fine filigree, hand-painted with great care.

'I think my chances have improved. The presentation beats the contents. If they get tired of reading they might pick the best cover.'

'No, Joe,' Kate hastened to reply. 'The cover conceals the masterpiece.'

'Like you under all those clothes.'

The cable tram had moved to them silently, and they were startled when the driver rang the bell to catch their attention. Once they were aboard, the tram accelerated and they were in the centre of the city in just a few minutes.

The *Bulletin*'s main office, printing and distribution were all in Sydney. A small advertising and referral office nestled in between the two large Melbourne newspapers. The artistic population and most other radicals either political or social were avid readers of the *Bulletin*. Its national circulation was far greater than the combined circulations of both Melbourne presses.

Joe and Kate were aware of this, and so it was with some pride that they accepted direction to the manager's office where Joe handed over his entry, which bore the *nom de plume* 'Warrigal Jack'.

Later, some tea was served by the *Bulletin* secretary. Kate noticed Joe's attentions towards this woman and detected an anxiety building within her. Joe suddenly had become shy and awkward towards Kate. He thanked her in a formal manner, feeling uncomfortable, for he could see she had noticed and was obviously put out. He would have persevered to right the situation, but his mind was also on John and his stripper waiting to be unloaded at the railyards. For a moment they were alone.

'I'll see you tonight.' Joe was not sure if he was invited a second night. 'I'll call by and take you to supper.'

Kate quickly saw his predicament. 'And you'll stay the

night then?'

'Oh, thanks.' Joe turned to her, kissed her as a father might his daughter, and left abruptly.

The railyards seethed with activity, horses and lorries manoeuvring in all directions, trains lying dormant like dead snakes being devoured by hundreds of ants. Joe soon found his train. The grain-stripper stood out among its cargo, the silver iron and red paintwork glistening in the midday sun.

It took some time for Joe to negotiate with a lorry driver to cart the stripper the half-mile to the showground site. Eventually Ben Murphy obliged, a young Irish immigrant more interested in the challenge of the job than the remuneration, or so it seemed. His lorry was the same level as the rail truck, so it was fairly easy to roll the stripper from one to the other. Once out at the site the stripper was lowered to the ground by a steam crane and moved to position among the competing exhibits.

Joe erected a small tent, then strung a banner across its side which announced in bold letters: 'The Furphy Grain-Stripper, with automatic height adjustment mechanism'. Inside the tent a trestle table became a pulpit for printed leaflets that advertised the array of other Furphy products. Joe breathed a sigh of relief, his task now complete, for John would arrive tomorrow in time for the judging next day. Joe pondered the likelihood that the *Bulletin* judging might take place at the same time.

The three judges had spent more time inspecting John's exhibit than they had other like entries. They seemed to be fascinated with the adjustment mechanism. John was not sure that they understood its workings and was undecided whether he should volunteer an explanation of this labour-saving device or risk disqualification for collaborating with the judges. He decided to restrain himself, remembering the

80

gospel teaching on the virtue of humbling oneself, so that in the event of being questioned by the judges his explanation would carry a strong message.

To his great relief he noticed that one of the judges obviously had some mechanical knowledge. He was explaining to the others by moving the lever then following the arm from the cutting combs through a series of bearings, a threaded ratchet that would wind through a clutch and finally to a cog, so that on release the lever would engage it to mesh with a large rim cog bolted to the inside rim of the stripper's wheel. Two of the judges still seemed apprehensive about the workings of this much-lauded invention, much to the annoyance of the more knowledgeable of the trio, who, throwing his arm in the air, beckoned to John to help with further explanation.

John was not confident that he could improve on the explanation already given and had decided that only demonstration would satisfy their doubt. He had in those few minutes approached two burly types who were passing by and explained that he needed to push the stripper a few yards. They seemed happy to oblige, sensing a chance to show off their strength to the small crowd watching. John introduced himself to the judges, indicating that he would be happy to demonstrate.

As he leaned forward, releasing the cog from the wheel by pushing the lever forward just as a combined weight of human mass moved the stripper into motion, John beckoned the judges to follow and when the stripper reached walking speed he pointed to the lever with one hand, then drew it back with the other. The cog meshed with the teeth on the wheel cog, and at that instant flashing shafts of forged steel whirred, and then amazingly, as promised, the cutting side of the machine lifted its hump back several feet into the air. John felt they were impressed with the mechanics of it but wondered if they understood its benefit. 'Sirs, this enables for quick height adjustment on uneven crops. There can be several bags to the acre saved by its use.'

The next day, when the winners were to be announced, was grey with a sleety rain. Across town a very different group of judges had moved from their studies and meeting rooms to join the press and a small gathering of academic types. To one side were the assembled entrants, all of whom were feeling less comfortable with those around them. Joe had said to Kate that it felt as though he was on an operating table, his parts dissected and inspected by doctors. It was always going to be as formal as possible, the surrounds of the room allowing nothing else. A speech by the *Bulletin* editor was followed by a speech from the Mayor, and then, to announce the winners, a professor of literature.

Kate was close to Joe, her arm curled comfortably through his. The announcement was brief: Joe had won the second prize. It was worth £5, and with it came a certificate, and the offer of publication of one of the stories in the *Bulletin*, on whose current front page was a patchwork of stamp-sized sketches of previous winners.

'Next year.' Kate was pointing, her short finger motionless with the determination and confidence of a hunting dog setting its prey. Joe wondered if he ever would join that clutch of élite.

The Centennial Exhibition had been an outstanding success, with more exhibits than other years, farm implements and a variety of produce reflecting a swing of interest from the goldfields and their decreasing yields to the prosperity of primary production for a hungry nation. The judges' dais was suitably decorated with flags of the British Empire and a large print of the Queen. Certificates and red-white-and-blue sashes were being presented by judges dressed in the finest tweeds. There was a pause in proceedings as new award sheets were handed out. There was some short appraisal by the judges concerned, then an announcement of the next section, that of the award for the most valued new implement. John had moved forward and to the side of the gathered crowd, confident that he might require easy access to the dais.

'Third Prize to Charles Smith & Sons from Ballarat for the Multi Size Chaff Cutter. Second Prize to Charles McKay and the Side Angle Hay Rake.' John was moving forward now. 'And First Prize to John Furphy Esq. for the Automatic Lift Stripper.'

John was on the dais. There was some applause that could barely compete with the noises of the surrounding show, but enough for John to wait for its lapse before he acknowledged the award with a few words on the wholesome grain and those that played a part in its ultimate harvest—this of course included the importance of mechanical assistance.

He was about to go on when he noticed Joe in the crowd and beside him that Kate Baker wench. He was shocked that Joe would so blatantly be seen with his lover—for word had gone around the family—even if it was in an anonymous city. Why at this moment? He stumbled for words, his concentration gone. John bowed his head in what many thought was simply a humble acceptance, then walked from the stage. His face, now hidden in the crowd, was contorted with rage. Joe, oblivious of his brother's consternation, went up to him, Kate still at his side.

'Congratulations, John. The folks back home'll be proud of you.' Kate nodded in agreement. Her hair now loosened by the wind was more becoming. John was aware of her presence but did not acknowledge her. He turned to Joe. 'When you get to Nagambie, leave the stripper at Parris Bros. It's sold. Load it on tomorrow's train.'

With that he turned, gathered his case, winning medallions and certificates, and strode off in the direction of the rail station. He arrived in time to catch the afternoon train on its return to Shepparton.

CHAPTER 10

Northward

AWAY FROM THE southern right-
eousness, the increasingly tight groups of the affluent and
religious who took it upon themselves to make the rules by
enclosing the town and its community in a halo of self-satis-
faction and parochial pride, Joe felt at ease up country,
working his team north of the Murray, up the Darling River.
Wool, which was normally transported by river barge down
the Darling to Wentworth, was now being hauled overland
by the teamsters. There was abundant work and good money
paid by wealthy pastoralists, who were favoured with a run
of good years in the 1880s. Now, in the early '90s, the
Darling was a series of stagnant waterholes, in places joined
by a thin ribbon of brown water that glistened silver in
reflected angles of sunlight.

It was twelve months since Joe had once again bade his
brother farewell, this time with a determination to prosper
as he had heard others had. Some he knew of had saved
enough to sell their team and start up business after a twelve
or eighteen-month stint. Besides, things had not been the

same between the brothers after that Melbourne trip. Leonie seemed to him happy enough with the routine life she and the boys were at ease with. This was much to Joe's consternation. He thought of taking Sam with him, but his conscience told him that his sons stood a better chance of being different from him if they followed their own path. They seemed able now to be independent of their father, and Joe accepted this with mixed feelings—pride at their confident exuberance and a sadness at the memory of those early years when their wide eyes soaked up his tales of the chances and dances of life.

Leonie had accepted his journey to the north with her usual indifference. The dull loneliness of her life had blunted even her anger towards him. Her only outlet now was Sherbourne's Inn a mere hundred yards up the street. She had at last conjured up the courage to visit it. The people were friendly, and there were strangers around to talk to. Memories flooded back of the days in her mother's hotel— she was now almost what her mother would have called a 'regular'. She knew that she was drifting into her mother's habits, and that those habits led to the back rooms of the inn. On rare occasions, and in discreet secrecy, she found solace in the arms of strangers.

Joe was sitting on the bank of the empty twisted river with its graveyard of fallen tree trunks. Two hundred yards upstream a waterhole reflected an upside-down river red gum, his team of bullocks stood idly beside it, content now with their bellies full of water. Around Joe were the branches of an old knotted gum with several saplings striking at its territory, their leaves a vibrant green, their limbs supple but spindly as they reached for light. Joe saw these as symbols of his sons, reaching away from the shadows of their parent, racing headlong into life but as yet unformed.

The old tree was now sprawling and bent by a hundred

storms; sections of its branches were dead, but still it held life. Reaching with crooked arms, it gathered Joe into its embrace. The warm sun filtered through until his drowsy mind joined to become the tree, now looking down on his sapling sons, content with their progress but troubled as his ageing limbs tried to hold a lifeless Leonie. The dream faded and he contemplated the inaccurate comparison, for his frame was not robust like the tree, rather it was lanky and bent at the top. Was this the reason, he wondered, that he could not embrace age as the river red gum could?

Joe tipped the tin mug, swinging his arm as if in two-up. A splat of tea leaves and stale brown liquid flattened on the red earth. Reaching for his pack, he tied the mug to it with a leather bootstrap that allowed it to swing freely. Twenty minutes later, the team moved off, heading north, staying parallel to the river but remaining a mile or so out to avoid the wash of gullies that widened close to its banks.

Over the last twelve months Joe had saved £340. It had taken eight trips north to south at varying distances, and now he had an offer from a teamster in Wentworth to buy his team of bullocks for £120. He was close to his target of £500, an amount that would allow him to buy a shop, an ironmonger's store with farm produce, as his father had back in Kyneton all those years ago. Leonie would sell the domestic hardware. It would be a new start for her too.

A lot depended on this trip. It was by far the longest and would take him beyond Wilcannia to the north, where stretches of sandy desert would appear as if stamped by lightning, fingers of barren sand laid bare of growth spearing at the edges of red earth.

Several desperate but wealthy pastoralists had offered £100 a load to transport their wool south to the Murray, and Joe had heard of the offer when last in Wentworth. He and at least three others had decided to take it up and had dispatched a letter with a mailcoach driver headed for Broken Hill via Wilcannia, giving their arrival and expected departure date with cargo.

It was of some concern that one of the largest teamster companies had considered the trip risky because of the lack of water in the Darling system. Joe had wondered if it was a genuine concern or simply an excuse to avoid a long trip that might have upset their service to existing customers.

Joe was pondering this as he approached the halfway mark. His beasts were as good as he had ever seen them. The waterholes, although becoming less frequent, were easily found and the feed was plentiful in the dried areas of the riverbed. There was at least four weeks' travelling to reach the stations and Joe was looking forward to the evening, for it had been prearranged with the other two teamsters who were travelling two or three miles apart to meet as they had done on each Saturday, and Joe had decided that he would ask a little more about just what they might expect further north. Both had been to the area and he was comforted by the fact that they spoke confidently of the task ahead. He would, however, be cautious to avoid showing concern in case they thought he doubted their judgment.

When night fell the blaze of the camp fire outlined three figures, sprawled at various angles to avoid smoke but remain comfortable. They had discussed the shearers' strike which was beginning to grip the country. They told yarns and to Joe's hidden satisfaction spoke confidently of the job ahead.

Next morning as Joe was about to lift the collar and place it over a bullock's head he hesitated, for his back was aching. He straightened, then bent one knee, then lifting swung it over the bullock's head. Then a slight downward push and the collar slipped into a fitted position against the beast's massive shoulders. The bullock seemed to relax—a beast of burden somehow satisfied, made comfortable—as a man on a cold day does by the donning of an overcoat.

Joe thought of Felix and Sam. They would be in his brother's foundry by now, content to lift heavy boxes of sand which would be rolled and lifted again thirty times a day. Like the bullocks, their labour had become a habit. If this trip worked as planned and he sold the team right, he might be able to set his boys on a new path, perhaps as salesmen and buyers for his produce store.

Cold Set

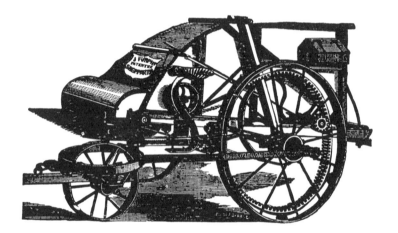

CHAPTER II

Rebel Plans

SAM AND FELIX had grown into strapping young men, Sam slightly taller with more of his father's build, Felix stockier but with shoulders wide and muscles that filled out a tight flannel singlet so that his body heaved with the rhythm of youth. Already Felix's skin was shining with sweat. He had been two hours striking for old Don the blacksmith, whose forehead and bald head showed small bubbles of sweat. Felix would watch fascinated as the bubbles lost their shape in the heat of the day, then join and roll to the furrows of his brow. Sam was on the moulding floor along with three others. Over recent months the moulding process was the busiest section of the factory, for there had been a change in production.

The stripper with all its forged parts and awards was suddenly taken out of production, a decision John had agonised over for some time. Should he continue to manufacture and sell this prestigious implement complete with its brass Centennial Award plaque riveted prominently to the front hopper, all the patterns and forgings, the specially made tongs and dies that created the shapes, over a year in preparation? Or should he accept the truth, that a better stripper had been invented in South Australia, one that would revolutionise the industry? It was a machine that had the ability not only to strip the wheat head but to thresh it, allowing the grain to be separated from the husk and be ready for bagging in one operation. The stripper was obsolete and John's decision had to be a business one.

Fortunately the timing was as good as the decision, for John had another product he was confident would outstrip the stripper, a product that would not be improved on by others. It was a product necessary to all farms: a means of carting water. He would call it the Furphy Water Cart.

The moulds on the foundry floor were now of a different shape. Replacing the stripper's square and rectangular shapes were four-foot circular moulds that were domed at the top, taking the shape of the backyard house well.

Sam and Ted were on the last of a two-day run of moulding. They had just two hours to complete the last four moulds and then be ready to cart molten iron to the thirsty moulds. It was heavy work, and Sam had said to Felix that it was not right that they should do this particular work week in week out while John's sons William, George, and recently Charles, all now employed with their father, seemed able to avoid the hard work. Particularly William and George, for Charles the youngest was considered slightly backward. He stuttered so badly that he had decided at an early age it wasn't worth the effort to talk; later when he had tried he couldn't, for an infection in his ear had rendered him stone deaf.

John had decided that Charles, who was good with his hands, would work at the new reaming lathe. It was a noisy operation that Charles would not hear as the machine scraped the inner walls of the cast-iron taps to a smooth tapered skin that would hold a watertight seal. A similarly machined brass plug was then inserted. John was proud of the expert production of these taps; it was they that delivered what he called the cart's 'wholesome contents'.

In the short space of time since ceasing production on the stripper, the manufacture of the water cart had come to dominate the entire factory. All sections were involved, the blacksmith's shop making steel bands, axles and wheels, the entire casting shop devoted to the tank end moulds and component parts, a woodworking section where shafts were shaped for the horse-drawn model, and finally an assembly area where a rolled cylinder and tank end came together held by the uncompromising forces of a steel band. Heated red-hot, its diameter expanded over the cylinder and end, then, on cooling, it squeezed them together, locking as it reduced circumference, never to let go. Old Charlie Newby, who was in charge of this job, had explained to Felix, who in turn told Sam, that the process was like having a good woman who 'opens hot, then locks, never to let go'. They had wondered if they should share it with William and George but decided not to as they were like their father and influenced by his preachings.

John was aware of his good fortune. The water cart had the potential to make him a fortune. Most days he would revise his sales and profit calculations. His aim was to take the level of production to twenty tanks a week, which would give him a profit of over £2,000 a year. By doing this John knew there would be no room for other manufacturers to encroach on his sales, as had happened with the stripper. He smiled with satisfaction, for a foundry with melting capacity was required to make the ends, and apart from his own, there were only such establishments in Melbourne and Sydney.

CHAPTER 12

Back to the
North

ROM A DISTANCE the wagons looked like moving pyramids, banks of red earth making a backdrop for the theatre of this travelling inland commodity on the start of its long journey to the ports of the world. The wagons were loaded in a high taper which seemed out of proportion with the area of their base. Eighty bales was considered a good load for a team of six bullocks. Joe's wagon carried ninety-six, the extra number a bonus for what was to be his last trip.

It was four days since they had each arrived in convoy at Smedley Station, and it was there that the two other stations had brought their wool so that it could be loaded at the one site. The owners of the various stations were also there to negotiate a final price and check the loading with the teamsters. Loch Bry Station was owned by a gentleman called Harris, obviously a Scotsman for he wore a kilt. He was a small man, but like many small men in the bush, he had a lot to say. He tended to think out loud about his business deals, but had the knack of keeping silent when it suited him.

Clarrie and Ben got the jump on Joe as usual. They immediately picked their individual choice. Clarrie went over to Wal Richards, the owner of Whyalla Station, a large jovial type more interested in the rare company of others than the all-important task of negotiating a price and striking a deal. Ben had been approached by Ryan from Kindale Station, who had noted that Ben was the strongest of the trio and that his team of bullocks seemed healthy and hardened. And that is how Joe was left with Harris. But Harris had picked his target, for he had detected a hesitation in Joe's demeanour, and calculated that an uneasiness in Joe's negotiation style was likely to follow, and that he could use all his cunning to swing a deal his way. The ability of Joe and his team to deliver was less important than the saving on pounds, shillings and pence that he would make.

When the contracts were finalised, Joe was quick to approach his comrades to compare deals. To his great surprise all three had been offered £90 a load, and all were required to leave a cash deposit of £100 with the owners, which would be refundable with the £90 at the Commercial Union Bank in Wentworth on safe delivery of the wool. Prices had obviously been determined before the meeting. Joe, relieved that all seemed equal, was about to start loading when Clarrie called him.

'What was your bonus, Joe?'

'Bonus?'

'Yair, Ben and I were offered an extra £20 if we could deliver to Wentworth wharf by August fifteen.'

Joe quickly read the detail of his contract. There was no mention of a bonus and he was required to deliver by the same date or else lose all payment and his deposit. On a closer comparison of the contracts it was found that Clarrie and Ben had an extra thirty days to September the fifteenth before they could lose their deposit and payment. All agreed that August the fifteenth was easily achievable. Joe was relieved that at least the timing seemed safe, and reluctantly accepted that he had missed a considerable amount in bonus, a 20 per cent reduction in what his mates stood to make.

The two owners had decided to pass on the extra price they would receive if the wool reached its destination at the earlier Melbourne sales when the product was not as abundant and therefore making a greater price. Harris had led them to believe he would do the same.

A comfortable night was spent at Smedley. After a hearty meal of roast beef and Yorkshire pudding, with apple pie to finish, they retired to a splendid room with deep leather couches. The fire blazing under the mantel relaxed their bodies; whisky and port sharpened their minds until the stories flowed—hidden tales from the back of the mind that kindled with the liberating wash of alcohol. There was a poem or two where it fitted, but only after Joe had lit his pipe and a gentle puff of smoke marked the pauses, relaxing and regenerating those other minds that had expended their contents in order to share the night. Later he gave them a two-day-old poem, not yet known by heart. It was penned in the evening at one of those waterholes and inspired by the throaty belch of a bullfrog. As it happened the paper with his ramblings was folded in his tobacco pouch, normally a haven for unfinished verses, that night an embryo of thought to be recited and shared.

The Bullfrog Bell

Now the truce of night brings respite to the sordid care of day,
  And in listlessness I pace the river side,
Where the solitude is wounded by no lighted window's ray;
  But illicit fancy will not be denied—

For the darkening flat reiterates a freer life's farewell
  In the long-familiar knocking of a bullfrog bell.

And in reverie I see the loaded wagons slowly creep
  Far across the western plains of New South Wales;
With 'talking' spokes and felloes, with wool-ropes biting deep,
  And the dust of two broad countries on the bales,
*Till the stars take shape in patterns, and through their
dreamy spell*
  Comes the low incessant knocking of the bullfrog bell.

And the retrospection lingers, bringing spiritless regret,
  Though the northward track is open to me still—
I may count the morning muster—I may track the stragglers yet—
  I may spell or battle onwards, as I will—
I may wake at night to listen, and know that all is well
  By the reassuring answer of the bullfrog bell.

But the virile life repeated would be wearisome and trite,
  Since the glamour of adventure cannot last.
When the Future, with its freshness, its pulsing roseate light,
  Has congealed into a leaden-coloured Past.
So an unreturning era owns its sympathetic knell
  In the melancholy knocking of that bullfrog bell.

After two days out on the return trip they had lost a day
when Ben's load moved and the entire load required restack-
ing. Joe considered continuing alone, but decided there
might be benefits in them sticking together. Besides, what if
the same happened to his load? He would lose more time if
out by himself.

What was of more concern was a mutual acknowledge-
ment of the reduced number of waterholes along the
riverbed. They had been careful to plot the watering sites on

the way up, for one dry hole ment a slower haul over twice the distance.

On the fourth day of their return trip their spirits had lifted as they were due to reach a substantial watering hole with good flat, heavily grassed areas. The river at this point took a long bend of about two miles' radius. It forfeited its depth to a shallow flat which flooded with the slightest rain. The drought had set in and the oasis of green had lost its visual impact, but the faded grasses still retained their nutritional value so that the entire area was habitat to an array of wildlife, and the wildlife enticed another type of predator who had also taken up residence.

It was late afternoon when the trio came in sight of the river bend. A haze of shimmering grey-green resolved itself into a belt of large trees which looked as if they were sitting on the red claypans in the foreground, whereas in reality their roots dug firmly into the rich soils of the river flat. And then, a little closer, Joe noticed that what had appeared to be small banks of cloud were in fact small fires, sending plumes of thin smoke snaking into the sky.

He was leading the others by half a mile now in an effort to give his team extra feed time. Now he decided to wait to confer with the others. Joe knew there could be trouble, that they had been beaten to the site by others, others that Joe knew had every right to use the land of their heritage. On this occasion, Joe expected his comrades to be enraged by the Aborigines and while he had often tried to go along with them, he knew that their beliefs and his would be at odds.

CHAPTER 13

Foundry Feuding

AT THE HISS of the whistle Sam and Ted, as if in some exercise routine, put hands on hips and arched their backs, the reverse to a bow that stretched the vertebrae of their spine and relieved the dull ache that was already setting in. It was morning break, a spell for ten minutes that John had finally allowed when convinced that other local manufacturers were obeying a law that their counterparts had accepted months before.

The best part for Ted was to roll a smoke, then inhale deep, for the smoke had a soothing effect on an anxiety deep down in his stomach. The exhaling smoke might relieve a pressure, then he might have the guts to follow through with his idea and make the suggestion to Sam that they should start their own foundry—a thought contemplated by the pair from time to time, a mischievous, daring dream that up till now was mocked as having no serious intent.

It was obvious that the firm was not keeping up with orders. For weeks now they had been making extra moulding boxes, a job that increased their workload, for the number of boxes determined the quota of moulds per cast. They now had forty boxes which produced forty tank ends every four days, and so production was set at twenty tanks every four days.

Ted drew on the thin, even fag, its only sign of fatigue a sponginess of the paper where it sat on his lips. Sam had often watched and admired the making of his weed, the very correct and even line of tobacco that was stretched onto the thin open paper, a nimbleness of thumb and fingers that worked gently on the tobacco strands until they fell into line, the thumbs then working, rolling until the paper cocooned its contents, a swipe of the tongue to seal, and finally more rolling to eliminate any small wrinkle or bulge. Then the lighting process, a total secret as it was performed in cupped hands.

Sam saw the same care and workmanship in his moulding technique. Together they had a minimal rejection rate of tank ends—they could make them with their eyes closed. As Ted took a last drag, then stamped it out, he started, a curl of smoke exhaling with the first few words.

'If they ask for more boxes to be made I'm refusing. We just can't go on making more. Even Dulcie said I better give up 'cause it's making me tired at night—honest, I fall asleep half an hour after I get home. Besides, we're not getting any extra for it.'

'Dulcie said we should take up her Dad's offer—to set us up with a shed behind his butcher's shop.'

'Look, Sam, I did some figures last night on costs. There's good profit in those tanks, and if we sold ten a week, with just the two of us, we could pay for setting up costs in one year and make good wages too. After that we might come up with some new lines.'

Sam was never at ease when Ted talked of this venture. After all, the water cart was his Uncle John's invention. So in order to cut short Ted's enthusiasm he said that he would talk it over with Felix that night, explaining to Ted that he would only be in it if Felix joined them.

A short blast of steam preceded the whistle that signalled a return to work.

As they returned to the work floor Ted was satisfied that Sam was at least tempted. John and William were waiting for them at the end of a row of moulds, as if this were a request for more boxes to be made. 'Look out,' muttered Ted.

William was first to speak. 'I need time with the tank end pattern to add some wording. Can you be finished with it by lunch time?'

There were eight ends to make. 'That means you want us to make eight in three hours. We've told you we can't do better than two per hour,' Ted blurted out, and then as if to ignore their presence he took his riddle and extended his reach over the moulding box as Sam directed a shovelful of black sand into its meshed base.

'Don't sieve that. Stop. Let's talk about this.' John was pushing past William, careful to avoid stepping on surrounding moulds. 'If you work through lunch break, we'll get the eight.' Then he added, 'You can knock off early tomorrow.'

'While you're pouring this arvo, William will be able to add the extra wording to the pattern.' John had turned and his voice trailed. 'There's a drought on up north. I'm expecting there'll need to be extra tanks made. We should help with the plight of the man on the land.' And then as always the pious comment: 'In the shelter of one's stable work place, one tends to forget others.' He had moved away now and Ted was careful to pitch his voice so that only Sam and, he hoped, William would hear it.

'There he goes, bloody preaching again. All very well, but what about the plight of his workers?' His eyes glared at William, who shifted on one foot, then, swivelling, faced

Ted, a drawn smirk on his face. Together Sam and Ted reached for their shovels and in unison shovelled the heaped sand into the box until it overflowed, then pounded the sand with rammers, each venting a pent-up anger.

In the late afternoon when the pour was completed, they went outside, chasing any breeze that might filter through their flannel singlets. Ted asked Sam if he and Felix could come to his house that evening for supper. Sam's reply was quick: 'We'll be there, eight sharp.'

CHAPTER 14

Slaughter at the River Bend

THERE WOULD HAVE been a hundred Aborigines, divided into small family groups. Clear patches of claypan among the fading grasses gave effect to an order, a type of early indigenous sub-division, excavated by wind and rain, the clay areas swept clean by the wind, small grass huts constructed in all shapes and sitting at odd angles.

They had spread themselves over the entire bend and Joe wondered if this was intentional in order to stake a claim on an expanse that would see them through the harshest drought.

The three teamsters were together now. Clarrie was quick to give his view, as if not prepared to contemplate their dilemma, implying in an offhand manner that the blacks should not be considered important.

'We'll lead the team down to the water and then let them feed where they like,' adding, 'we'll camp at the water's edge.'

Ben nodded agreement, then said, 'But are they likely to object and even threaten us?'

'Not while we've got this.' Clarrie had reached under the wagon seat and had withdrawn a double-barrel Scott & Wembley shotgun.

'Perhaps we should talk to them first. They might shift, or make some room.' Joe was pointing to a group of men who had gathered in the foreground.

'There's no bloody point, Joe, but come on if it'll satisfy you two.' Clarrie moved ahead of the others, impatient, with a determined, almost military approach, the gun held across his body so that the late afternoon sun gleamed a dull sparkle on its barrel.

There were signs of the effect of a prolonged drought on those who stood before them. They were lean, with skin sunk over a broad bone structure, once proud hunters of the endless plains, now confined to river bends, hills and poorer country not yet taken up by the squatters and pastoralists. Their eyes were large and silent. Clarrie was forward of the other two now, so that his chest was only a foot from the foremost Aborigine, the gun in between, and yet they remained serene, like black lambs to the slaughter, Clarrie thought as he broke the silence.

'We have to water and feed our team.' He pointed to the three wagons and the listless bullocks still harnessed, relieved at first to be motionless, their heads fallen to relieve the weight on their shoulders. Before Clarrie could continue, they were gestured to an area on the other side of the riverbed. There was limited feed there, as the banks rose to the desert plain level in a narrow strip about ten yards wide.

'We can't restrict them to that small strip.' Ben was talking now. 'We have no fencing to keep them confined.' He hesitated now as he realised they did not understand, then going down on one knee he drew a shape of the river bend on the claypan, dots depicting cattle on the suggested strip of river bank, then a series of trailing arrows suggesting that the bullocks could move anywhere. The four Aborigines considered the drawing for a long time. Clarrie, losing patience, beckoned Joe and Ben to leave them.

'Just let's look after ourselves.' He turned to walk away, when Joe explained they should wait, for he knew that these people needed time. It was part of their culture. Besides, to them time was of no consequence. It was ten more minutes before they sat in a circle and commenced their drawing. The snake-like bends of the river bank were exact, and the detail of their camps placed with pinpoint accuracy. One of them was more fussy than the others and insisted in smoothing the fine dust in order to erase and redraw in greater detail.

Eventually they shuffled into a squatting position and beckoned the teamsters to join them on the ground. Joe was quick to oblige, kneeling on two knees and resting on his ankles. Ben remained on his feet but squatted, allowing his knees to protrude at ungainly angles; Clarrie simply craned his neck and peered down.

The plan before them was simple, but not possible. It depicted the bullocks still on the high bank and still in harness, the rear two a pivot for the others, for they were tethered on a long lead tied to a tree. Small arrows indicated the circular movement of their feeding pattern. Clarrie scoffed, 'Shows you what they bloody know about animals.' He started to walk back to the wagons. Joe tried to explain to them that it would not work, using his hands to show how the bullocks would become hopelessly tangled. They seemed not to understand. The meeting was breaking up and Joe could think of nothing more that might hold them together.

Clarrie's booming voice shattered the tension of their quandary: 'HOO—Yraaaa', followed by a gathering rumble as the bullocks gathered speed, their nostrils flared as they

107

sucked in the smells of the muddy waterhole. There was a scatter of women and children running to hold each other as the bullocks bolted through the camp, then a calm again as the beasts wallowed in the brown water, drinking as they waded into its cool depths.

Joe was furious. He agreed that the bullocks needed to be fed and watered, but there was a way of leading them to it.

It was almost dark when Joe led his team to the water-hole. Reluctantly he had also decided that the bullocks should roam free in the river bend. There seemed no other option, and besides, they required maximum food intake for the next leg of the journey.

There was little discussion around the camp fire that night. Clarrie and Joe had their differences, but this latest episode was the final straw. Ben had sided with Clarrie, his security somewhat more assured with this extroverted partner. That night Joe offered some damper to a group of camp children. They took it and ran off to their huts, and Joe was never sure if they ate it, or if they did, whether they enjoyed it.

Joe had decided to leave by midday the next morning. Clarrie and Ben would take an extra day to spell their teams. They had the luxury of extra time, and Joe knew he was already one day behind schedule.

The morning broke with a stretch of sunrise on the horizon, its colours challenging the reds and browns of the plains that at a distance arched to join as one. The Aborigines seemed very quiet, and on closer examination Joe found that the huts were in fact empty. He scanned the river bend, his hand shielding his face from the low ball of sunlight. There was no sign of anyone. Clarrie appeared from his tent and after some coughing and farting he too noticed that the camp was abandoned.

'There now, you see, Joe? They move like crows. They'll

be back when we've gone, see?'

Deciding not to continue a confrontation, Joe ignored him. Instead he was looking at the bullocks. They certainly had appeared to pick up overnight. They were spread over the entire bend and as a matter of habit Joe was picking his bullocks from the others. He seemed to be two short. His eyes narrowed as he scoured the area again. This time he located one other. He was less concerned now, for the last one was bound to be there among the others. He turned to Clarrie and Ben. 'Those bullocks look good, eh?' He had decided to get back on speaking terms with them.

He poked at the camp fire. Red ash glowed then faded, a bed of white ash still hot underneath, the flame having been exhausted overnight. Then he dumped a handful of dry gum leaves in its centre. One leaf carried a huge ant which crawled onto the ash in an attempt to escape, but the hidden heat overcame it as it curled into a ball, changing colour to become part of the ash. The leaves were smouldering now. Sudden combustion dissipated the smoke in a gush of orange flame.

Again Joe cast his eye over the grazing bullocks, this time slowly. He knew all the bullocks in Clarrie and Ben's team too, and still he was unable to locate one of his team. He counted them all, starting from one end of the bend, careful not to double-count, then he counted again, and both times he got a total of fifteen. There should have been eighteen. Joe was getting annoyed with himself now. Was he simply miscounting? Was one beast hiding another? He poked at the fire and added some heavier sticks, then he marked off the first letter of the name of each beast in his team. Helmut was missing, his rear leftsider, the plodder that took the weight of the wagon before the others when the wagon encountered an incline or deep gutter. He noticed too that Clarrie was missing his lead bullock and

Ben his centre right.

Joe felt some relief, knowing that three were missing, for there would be safety in numbers. One could have led the others, but where? He scanned the horizon. There was nothing but a haze of growing heat that would soon shimmer as the sun climbed overhead. On the other side of the river his view was unhindered. Could they be lying behind the huts protected from the early glare of sun? He walked over, looking behind each hut. As he approached what appeared to be the head man's hut he noticed a discolouring on the clay, a mass of flies swarming on congealed clots. It was blood.

Then he saw them, three bullock heads sitting upright in the sand, their eyes wide open, a dull, sorrowful expression remaining after death, their nonchalant demeanour unable to understand the fading of life as their hearts pumped a gush of blood from their severed necks. Joe felt a knot in his throat that momentarily choked off his breath, then he moved closer trying to identify Helmut, annoyed at first for not immediately recognising his own, for minus their bodies all three looked identical. A spongy growth under Helmut's eye, a cancer that one day would have taken his life, was Joe's way of knowing him.

Eventually he waved to the others to come over, and while they did he realised the enormity of the problem it was going to cause. Ben was devastated. He put his arm on Joe's shoulder, and together they mourned those beasts of burden. Clarrie went into a rage. His first reaction was to chase after those 'black murderers of the night', as he described them, for this was premeditated, planned in the daylight, for how else would they have managed to kill one from each team?

Half a mile to the west, dark dots appeared, circling on a backdrop of blue sky, then some dropping to the ground to feed on the offal and other beastly remains. The skins and large cuts of meat, the most valuable to the Aborigines, were now miles away with them to the north, the opposite direction to that in which the teams were travelling.

Now time was more precious than ever. One bullock less would slow the teams, unless they were driven harder. They were almost at capacity speed now, but they would have to do better. Joe decided to leave immediately. He bade his comrades farewell and good luck, realising that from here on he was by himself. After readjusting the harness to make up for Helmut's absence, Joe set off in the midday sun, his plan to travel all day and through the night. He had time to make up and one less beast to carry the load.

CHAPTER 15

The Last Straw

TED'S WIFE WAS a good cook. Her dropscones and coffee and the cosy interior had set the mood for relaxed conversation which lasted while supper was served. It finished when Ted placed sheets of well-worn writing paper across a recently cleared table and turned up the kerosene lamp, its light setting a new atmosphere that would accompany the harsh reality of decision-making.

The costing sheets showed land and buildings at no charge. Other costs totalled £1,605. The largest single cost was for furnace, blower and lifting winch, which together would be £549. Another major cost was for a load of special sand from Melbourne at £220. This would act as a base sand to which other local sands could be added at a fraction of the cost. The manufacture of moulding boxes was minimal, for Ted had devised a method of using the steel rims from old wagon wheels and had collected them in anticipation. He had sufficient for fifteen complete moulds and that would amount to seven tanks each pour.

On the income side, sales were based on three pours per

week which would result in up to twenty-one tanks per week less any rejects. A figure of fifteen tanks was estimated as achievable from a production angle. The figure was further reduced to ten tanks per week as a conservative sales estimate. The bottom line showed sales of 500 tanks at £12, which equalled £6,000.

Total costs for the year were itemised as: set-up £1,605; all running costs £2,275. This included their wages and left a modest profit of £120 for their first year. Sam noticed the selling price of the water cart at £12. His Uncle John was selling his at £14. The difference was significant, and he felt a joyous fear, mixed with guilt in the knowledge of what effect this could have on John's operation. Felix could not contain his excitement. He was quick with figures, and if the enterprise were to take off he would be the obvious choice as bookkeeper.

Ted had moved to the fireplace. 'This don't allow for extra castings we can make, wheels and hubs and so on. Ya have to admit the figures look good.' They were indeed good, and for a moment Felix wondered if he might have miscalculated. He had quickly added both sides of the ledger and was satisfied nothing had been missed.

Sam went over to Felix spontaneously, for he wanted to be seen to be speaking for his older brother. 'It looks good, Ted, but there are two things. First, without us there it will really affect production.'

'Till they train a couple more moulders,' Ted was quick to reply.

'And second,' Sam continued, 'where does this leave Dad? You know he relies on John for work.'

'Well, you'll have to work that out. He can work with us anyway, 'cause I need an answer by the end of the week. If not I'll start it myself.'

Friday came round quickly, and both Sam and Felix

were still hesitant. They could see an opportunity. If ever they needed to talk to their father it was now.

It was knockout morning and the silvery grey tank ends stood in the sand alongside the broken sand moulds that had earlier shaped their outer sides. Now chunks and lumps of sand lay spent, like cocoons or broken eggshells devoid of their contents. The sand would soon have the attention of shovel and sieve, then be firmed with additives of bentonite and plumbago as it was heaped into rows ready to produce again.

John and William were inspecting the ends as they stood propped in the sand. They moved down the rows as if conducting a military parade. Sam and Ted waited for the inspection to finish, for they knew there was going to be trouble. William had added extra wording to the tank end on the afternoon that Sam and Ted had worked through their lunch. The valuable wooden pattern had been laid out on a table in his father's office. A strong light was directed over it, and the painstaking job of carving lettering into its surface began. It took all afternoon, all night and part of the next day before the pattern was ready once again for the production of moulds. John was agreeable to the additional wording, for up till now the writing on the tank end had a distinctly commercial purpose. The name, 'J. Furphy—Maker—Shepparton', and a list of his other products adorned the end, fanning out on the domed surface, and now at the centre bottom, just above the location of the tap, were the words:

Good, better, best,
Never let it rest
Till your good is better
And your better best.

William had discovered the rhyme in an English machinery catalogue as part of an advertising slogan for the Wiltshire Lathe & Machinery Company of Birmingham. He had read it to his father, who was delighted that one of his sons appreciated the written word, especially words that carried a moral message. John had used the rhyme often in sermons, carefully placing the emphasis on the last word in each line. It fitted beautifully and rounded off almost anything he said. His growing admiration for William over George and Charles was obvious, and when William suggested that the rhyme should be spelt out on the tank end and George protested, saying that this would be pontificating, John insisted that it was appropriate to emblazon a part of their sermon on company products.

The inspection continued, more slowly now. John looked devastated. There was something badly wrong with those ends, all in a line, ready to be rolled to the fettling shop but now on a different route, to the scrapheap.

William turned to his father from the furthest row, and indicated that they were all the same.

'One hundred per cent reject rate,' John boomed, as he swung to face Sam and Ted. Felix was there too, for the knockout process required that all staff help. Closer inspection of the ends showed several small elongated holes that cut through the metal, leaving it worthless. Sam and Ted had noticed the holes first. They were looking for them. Experienced in the flow of molten metal, they had observed that William had carved his lettering into the pattern deeper than the existing writing. As far as William was concerned, the wider and deeper the V-shaped cut went, the more visible would be the wording, and William wanted this to stand out.

Before moulding with the newly inscribed pattern, Sam had suggested to William that his cut was too deep, that he might have created a problem with the metal running over such a thin section; William seemed doubtful of Sam's judgment, so to emphasise the point Sam continued to explain how the molten metal dulled and started its process of solidifying as soon as it left the ladle. Because the area of the mould was large, thirty-six inches in diameter, and the thickness a little more than a quarter of an inch, any further reduction in thickness might stop the flow of metal. Sam then suggested a solution, that the grooves be filled slightly with beeswax, so as to be sure they would turn out. William's pride was hurt. He explained, without really knowing the technical details, that they should make the metal hotter. And so it was that the full quota of moulds was made.

John moved closer to the moulders, then spoke with a calm voice that held each word, ensuring maximum penetration, as if talking to one a little dumb or slow of hearing, a practised style that he used in his sermons when describing the ways of a wilful sinner. His face was close to them now, so close that Sam noticed the uneven trim of moustache where it joined a silver beard. The top lip, normally covered, was a contrasting pale pink, and now it quivered with fury.

'William told me that you knew of the possibility of these ends not being satisfactory, and that you would not allow him time to fill the lettering with beeswax, an action that may have avoided this catastrophe. I'll lose sales unless they can be remade for a pour the day after tomorrow. I expect you'll need to work till midnight both nights to get the moulds down.'

William was beside his father now. Well trained, he took his father's stance, one foot lifted onto a box, his arms folded. 'Well, will you be agreeable then?' He hoped this would be the end of it, but it wasn't.

Sam and Ted moved closer, within striking distance.

'You rotten bastard!' Ted was the first to speak, but didn't go on. Rather he lowered his head in what came across as a genuine disgust in those opposite him.

Sam was furious. His cousin had twisted the truth so as to make it look as if they had caused the defects. 'I can't work with you any more. I'm leaving, now.' He threw down his shovel.

Ted was taken aback, but then a faint smile squeezed from the edges of his mouth and his eyes narrowed. 'Me too.' Then moments later, 'Me too' again. It was Felix, and he was following them to the foundry door. When they walked into the failing afternoon light it was as if a new day was dawning. All three had made up their minds about starting their own foundry.

That night Sam and Felix received a visit from their uncle. They were prepared, steady but nervous, in case they had to withstand John's mighty powers of persuasion. Leonie had agreed with her sons' decision, and took it upon herself to defuse the meeting. She met John at the front door, politely but with a stove poker held firmly in her hand. John opened his mouth to speak then saw what she held. He turned on his heel without a word and strode off, balancing on the narrow path between the spiky hands of the rose bushes. Inwardly he seethed, the demons of his anger now in full possession. Aloud—but when out of hearing distance—he cursed his brother's motley mob of fools.

Straight Pein

CHAPTER 16

The
Waterhole

JOE HAD MADE good progress since he left the site of the bullock massacre. It had been three days and he had just made camp at a small waterhole. So far his luck was in, for he had found water on each day, which had reassured him that he had made the right decision on the route he should take.

There were two tracks to Wentworth, one of which stayed well out from the Darling. It was a direct line 'as the crow flies', Clarrie had said. 'That's how we'll head home.' The other track followed closer to the river, and as a result the distance was greater, but it did have the advantage of waterholes and better feed in the bends. Joe had decided to play safe, and if all went well he should be there by the deadline eight days from now.

The camp site was perfect. A large river red gum provided shade. The smoke from the camp wound its way over the large limbs and thin foliage above, an incense of the tree's old growth now floating and caressing the new growth as it drifted skywards. Three bullocks had moved from the cool muddy waters to eat the grasses along the bank. The other two remained in the waterhole to ease their tight muscles and sinews. Twilight turned to darkness, and with it Joe's thoughts went to the times ahead when the trip would be over, his team sold, and the boys working with their mother in their new hardware shop. His more frequent trips to Melbourne, the completion of his book, and Kate, dear Kate. For she would advise him. To hell with editors and critics. Kate would work with him. Their minds and bodies could join to provide a powerful message to the do-gooders of the day.

Lawson and Paterson portrayed the battlers as somehow less successful, emphasising their quaint, earthy habits, fodder for the city dwellers who relished the tales of their unlucky country cousins. Miners, drovers, shearers, in the eyes of city folk, all lacked their affluence and their sophistication. Paterson and Lawson played on this and could barely keep up the supply of written material for the city customer.

Joe would embarrass them, reverse the story so the joke was on them. Subtle innuendo that would prick their consciences, but not enough for them to reject the book, for the publishers would be looking at sales. This is where Kate could best help him.

Joe fell in and out of sleep. Words were coming to him, but as in the past he would not remember them in the morning. Besides, he had a job to finish. He was woken by the birds, for they too had clustered in the vicinity of the waterholes—magpies and kookaburras, the first to herald the morning light. By the time Joe had swilled the last of his billy tea, only the drone of the crow remained, his shiny black feathers absorbing the increasing heat from the sun to create an energy within him to call louder and louder as the day went on, unlike the other species who were already finding shelter, and conserving energy simply to get through the day.

Joe glanced across at the bullocks. Two were feeding on the diminishing grasses, one was drinking from the edge of the waterhole, and two were in the water. As Joe went for the rope halters he glanced back, surprised that they seemed so low in the water, for it was unusual for bullocks to remain in water deep enough to cover their lower body. They were like the fully laden barges that plied this river at high level, down with a water mark at their flanks. As he approached he remembered that two bullocks had been in the hole the evening before.

He quickened his pace and came to the water's edge. There was something wrong. Could they be bogged in the mud? He was momentarily relieved when, as he waded to knee depth, the bullocks seemed content. The tops of their backs were dry, and their eyes reflected the untroubled serenity of the water. Then Joe remembered that same look in the lifeless eyes of their slaughtered team-mates just days before. He tried to reassure himself, but knew that those muddy waters were hiding what he feared most, and when he got to waist deep he knew what it was, for his feet were sinking deeper into the cool grip of heavy sludge.

He retreated a step or two after he had haltered the closest of the bullocks, Aladdin. The beast's pure black coat shone above the faintest yellow ripple of innocent, life-giving water; but the muddy depths had tightened around the legs, so that now there was no movement. Statue-like, the beasts were not uncomfortable; like their slaughtered fellows, they were unaware of their predicament. Joe was by now only too well aware of it, for as he pulled on the halter only Al's neck stretched.

Joe was not a strong swimmer, but now he had stripped to his underwear and dog-paddled out to put the halter on

Rupert, his lead bullock. Before returning to shore he duck-dived. Pulling himself down as he clasped at Rupert's lower shoulder and leg, his hand slid into the mud, which, loose on top, packed with a greater intensity as his fingers pushed down along the leg. They were down to their bellies in it, their legs fixed like piers under a jetty. Joe suddenly realised the extent of the problem: they could not move and without them, he would not move.

He decided to try again. This time he harnessed the three remaining bullocks, then paddled out again, the trace between his teeth. This attempt was unsuccessful, for the power of the bullocks pulling at their team-mates would have eventually throttled them. Again Joe paddled out, this time relocating the trace to underneath the front legs, up over the shoulder and around the lower neck. Now he was more hopeful. Taking the strain so as to alleviate any jolt, he calmly coaxed his depleted team to take up the tension.

Eventually when he was sure some part of the trace was about to break, the stranded bullock moved. Free at last from the suction, with a small ripple preceding the mass of flesh, the bullock came quickly through the water to the edge of the waterhole. But it did not stand. It lay motionless on its side, its lower body covered in a layer of yellow-brown mud.

Joe moved quickly, scraping the mud away. There were no cuts; the flesh was undamaged. His hopes rose. He was about to leave it and go to the other stranded bullock when he saw that the front leg tucked under the muddy body was at a peculiar angle. It took all his strength to roll the beast, and when he did he discovered that the hopelessly twisted leg was broken. He shuddered at the thought and knew that it was the angle from which it was pulled that had snapped the bony limbs—limbs which always seemed out of proportion to the bulk of these beasts.

Suddenly Joe's strength drained, and he slumped momentarily, utterly exhausted. The bullock, now without the cast of compacted mud, had feeling slowly coming back into its limbs. It tried to stand, its three good legs kicking to secure a hold, half standing, then collapsing again, and then the pain coming over it as the broken leg twisted hopelessly under the falling weight. It bellowed now, a low pathetic bleat, terror in the once tranquil eyes.

Again he dog-paddled to the remaining bullock, and diving, soon realised that this one could not be secured with a rope, for it lay deeper in the mud. Returning to the bank, broken now, Joe fell to the ground. He wept, not for the predicament that would surely see his contract lost, but for his two friends in pain, pain that would need to be stopped, that only death could shut out.

Unlike most teamsters, Joe did not carry a gun. The thought of cutting their throats was grotesque, for they would see their master inflicting more pain, as the blood took its time to drain through their strong hearts. The grounded bullock again tried to stand, as a newborn animal, half up, half down. With a sway that defied the forces of gravity, the newborns always made it, but this one wouldn't. Joe needed to do what he had to do, but how?

The remaining bullocks stood harnessed. The grass and water intake had swelled their stomachs. They could not know the fate of their team-mates, and as Joe contemplated their nonchalant serenity the method of execution came to him. Backing up the team, he slipped a halter that with a little alteration had become a noose over the head of the stricken animal, then with an urgent 'Yaa!', the depleted team moved forward. Five quick steps were required to gain movement with a wagon behind, a jolt that started the slow rotation of wheel, until the momentum allowed them to extend their stride, and five quick steps was all it took to choke their mate Al to unconsciousness before the neck snapped. Rupert was given the same treatment. He lay in a grave of mud, the murderous substance shining like new granite while damp, then drying hard, a token cover that would soon split in the heat of the sun and reveal its treasure to the patrolling carrion-eaters, forever watchful of those who had fallen.

Some time later, much later, for he was undone with sorrow, Joe had hitched his team to the wagon and left in the direction not of the river route but straight across the plains, at right angles to his planned route. He had decided that his only hope was to meet with Clarrie and Ted who had chosen the inland route. He hoped they would still be behind him when he got there.

CHAPTER 17

Maisie's Innermost Thoughts

IN THE EARLY 1890s the township of Shepparton was beginning to outgrow its neighbouring town of Mooroopna, three miles to the west. John's business grew with the town, and its increased output added its pressure to the many demands on his attention. His involvement with the Water Trust was at a peak, for he had been elected chairman of the Board, and he found the decisions on pipe-laying and pumping installations a daunting responsibility. As well as all this, his Sunday congregation was getting larger and his preparation time for sermons took longer. There were rewards for all this, not least his growing standing in the community, but he was beginning to feel that so much activity was beyond him, and that perhaps it was time to let go of some of it.

The abrupt departure of three of his key staff gave him just such an opportunity to rearrange his priorities. With his foundry John had two options: to continue to rule in all areas of the business, or to accept that it was time to hand the business over to William, allowing him more time to give to his wife and a congregation that still remained in awe of his eloquent preaching.

To his great surprise he decided on the latter, but the process of handing over control would need to take two or three years, which would give him time to install William as the head of the company but see his own methods and procedures maintained. William was the obvious choice, for like his father he lived the business, even when away from it. George was less inspired by the work routine and John had noticed that he was prone to laziness, doing only what was expected of him. Charles was a good steady worker whose hearing and speech impediment had a valuable side effect, for it enabled him to work in the noisiest section of the works. The noise of the lathe did not matter to Charles. He could not know that its relentless screech was exacerbating his problem to the point where his ears would ache at night.

Now that John had set himself a plan, he felt a zeal grow within him. There was a matter that required urgent attention, for William had heard that his cousins Sam and Felix together with Ted Newby were going to start a new foundry in Mooroopna with the sole intent of producing tank ends for the manufacture of their own water cart.

This was not the first time his inventions had been copied. His wagons and his grain-stripper were being produced by ex-employees, further up north, for they could be made with timber and iron forgings. But the thought of a competing foundry with the capability of cast iron production meant that his entire range was susceptible—not only the water cart but other important items such as a horse-works, round pig-feeders, and a host of wheels and hubs.

Somehow he had to stop them before they went any further. He decided that his first approach must be to his brother Joe, whose influence on his sons was respected. If that failed there was always the opportunity to make a financial offer that Joe could not resist. He would need to await Joe's return, convinced that the new foundry was at this stage only an idea. In the meantime he would find out more detail, such as just where they intended to set up. There might be a chance that he could make a counter-offer for land which might jeopardise the project before it began.

Sam and Felix had told their mother of the new venture and sworn her to keep it secret. John could not approach her after his last venture to her door, and in any case they had for years barely talked to each other. But there could be a way, for if there was someone in this town who might be able to find out it would be Maisie Sheppard, the widow of the local innkeeper, and surprisingly, given her close liaison with the town drinkers, one of his staunchest parishioners. Leonie often drank at Maisie's Punt Inn, sometimes a little too much. Somehow he would arrange a meeting with Maisie, but just how was not going to be easy, for she was the approachable type, only too approachable.

The Punt Inn was at one time the only drinking establishment in the town and until recent years had a shared use, for it was the residence of the punt operator and a meeting place for travellers who sometimes stayed overnight after the punt crossing. The inn was directly up the bank from where the punt used to cross. At that point the bend in the river allowed easy access on a gentle slope to the water's edge, and from the inn, views in two directions upriver enhanced the location. The crisscross of a wooden bridge lay across a narrow straight section two hundred yards downstream. The airborne structure had made the floating punt obsolete, and it lay at its moorings, the thick ropes that once hauled it from side to side no longer coiled neatly each side of the feeder drum but abandoned like some grotesque necklace hurriedly thrown onto a bedside table. A new hotel had opened, of substantial brick and iron lace, and it was here that most of the established gentry gathered.

The Punt Inn, though old, with low doorways and many rooms, competed well with its new rival, for it had one very prominent attraction, that of Maisie Sheppard. Her husband Sherbourne had died two years ago. As punt operator, he was usually the first person travellers would meet on arrival. He was popular, and although not prominent as perhaps other more wealthy citizens, he was the type that could influence the majority. He was in fact a sort of unofficial mayor, and when he died Maisie took over this role very successfully, for she had an added advantage with the men-folk in town.

Her prominence in the local Methodist Ladies Guild was so strong that John felt that she would give sermons if allowed. There were those in that same congregation who despised her, never able to reconcile the contradiction of her business with the strict anti-liquor teachings of their church. But that was not all, for the clothes that she flounced around in were more fitting to those behind the bar, and to women of younger years. Maisie was proud of her figure and moved with an assurance that gave her choice of apparel the desired second look, or was it what it concealed and revealed?

No one noticed this more than John, particularly from the vantage point of the pulpit each Sunday. The half-moon bosoms rose above the congregation, a distraction of heaven-ly movement that would inspire him to such fervour that the layman's natural urges rose to assert themselves within this Sunday preacher. The view got better with each step up the pulpit until the swell of breathing flesh below was separated only by elevation, a privileged position that was his alone.

He had often wondered if Maisie was aware of what she revealed, for she was always careful to sit in the same aisle seat, third back from the front, which was perfect, for it gave John enough elevation and yet obviated to some extent the downward glance that would have occurred had she been in the front row. Then there was the way she shifted, as if to make herself more comfortable. The real intention, John secretly imagined, was to offer even greater exposure. Even while he prayed 'Lead us not into temptation', he found himself thinking of what lay below the neckline of Maisie's dress. His frequent anger was something he could stifle into control, but not this. But he could scourge the demon drink out of his flock, and perhaps the good God would excuse him.

On this Sunday John had decided to approach her after the service, for it was his custom to talk with his congregation, a chance to get some response to his sermon. With Maisie he would have to arrange a meeting alone, and that could not be done after the service for people tended to approach him in groups—they stood in such awe of him that they found safety in numbers.

He had decided that to meet at the inn would invite comment from his conservative flock. He would arrange to meet her at the church hall this evening, and when he finally singled her out from the group his excuse for the meeting was that they should review the role of the women's guild, for it was common knowledge that the men of the church were feeling increasingly threatened. She gave him a look of concern at first, feeling she might be out of favour for she was a prominent member of the guild. But then close to her he seemed mortal, a man at her level, a man she might oblige.

John arrived first and waited in the side lobby entrance. Maisie would have the key. He hoped she would not arrive late, for although he was secluded from the passers-by, the side path was a short cut to the river bank used by children.

He was beginning to wish he had brought his key when Maisie suddenly and quite silently appeared. There was a contradiction about her which intrigued and excited him: the outwardly fervent demeanour he could see on her face at prayer, her devoted care for her church duties, but within a sultry devil, a breathing Satan that had welled up in her with every step on that short walk from the inn. The devil by now had her breathing short and deep, her breasts heaving and taking up the slack in her low-cut blouse. He followed her inside.

'Well John? I know there's been a clash with times here with the men wanting absolute priority on their meeting dates, but they won't organise regular meetings, which means our regular guild meetings often clash.' She turned to face him, at the same time sitting on a solitary chair that had been conveniently left away from the rows of chairs neatly stacked along the wall. Then looking up, her body now in a familiar position, she continued, 'So I've made up a roster. It's the only way this will work.'

'All right, I'll put it to the men.' He was glad to have that out of the way. He took the opportunity to retrieve another chair from the row along the wall. It was important that he not be distracted. 'There is one other matter, Maisie. Leonie Furphy is a good woman. She's had to battle with Joe and all. I fear Joe's boys may be embarking on a venture that will take what little they have, and with Joe away, I was hoping you could find out—to protect the family, mind you—just what the boys are up to and where they're going to locate their new business in Mooroopna, just so's I can check they're not paying too much for it. Now I know you get on well with her. She may tell you. Unfortunately she doesn't seem to like me, so I'm asking you.'

There was a silence, then she rose slowly up from the chair, a movement which gave elasticity to her body. At full height the curve of her hip was close to his face as she twisted from that same hip to look at him. Quickly John rose too, then she touched his shoulder. 'You're a good man John. I'll find out what I can.'

Her hand remained. It was not the sort of gesture which needed to linger, nor one that simply accompanied her response. It held there gently until the demons did their work, until John plunged his right hand down firmly on her heaving bust, his fingers spreading in order to cover as much of the bulging white skin, to claim it for as many seconds as it would last.

She seemed unsurprised, calm even, allowing all those sermons with their hypocritical morals to fade between them. Hands so practised at gesture to enhance the word of God, inventor's hands that felt the cold hard forms of his iron forgings, now caressed the firm soft swell of flesh until the nipples held in alluvial folds and crevasses hardened. Nuggets of gold that could no longer hold their secret, they protruded, inviting caress. It was a long time since those first few child-bearing years that John and his wife had touched, a guilty, hesitant touch that they had both decided was too uncomfortable to pursue.

On the next Sunday Maisie came alongside John after the service. She had information for him and was hoping that they might meet again that night. The last week had been a nightmare for John, for he was racked with guilt, and decided there would be no more meetings alone with Maisie. He was thankful that his act of lustful fondling had gone no further. With fury he thought of her unashamedly rearranging her clothes, accompanying him down the path to the street and smiling when they parted as though nothing had happened. And now she was beside him again, smiling that same smile.

He gestured Maisie to one side away from a group nearby. 'You can tell me now, Maisie.' She was about to, then hesitated, for this was not the time or place she had planned.

'John, I'd rather we talked alone about this. It's fairly sensitive.' Then after further pause and the shift of body she was so good at, she continued. 'Besides, I would not be prepared to divulge private matters about others in the church grounds.' John could not argue with this.

'All right, I'll meet you tonight as before.' He turned to rejoin the others, quietly cursing his ineptitude with women.

He had started the day well with a most successful sermon, and during the rest of that day he allowed it to elevate him to a righteousness above those around him, until he felt a power of almost godly proportions, sufficient to hold at bay any earthly temptations.

So when they met, same place, same time, Maisie was crushed, for the expectation of a manly follow-on of events did not occur, but rather this pompous, pious bastard suggesting she must mend her ways. Worst, he had first got from her the things he wanted to know about Leonie.

Maisie never sat in that same row on Sundays again. She moved to the rear of the church and joined the all-male choir.

Top Fuller

CHAPTER 18

Rescued

JOE HAD ESTIMATED that a distance of
up to eight miles should bring him to cross the old Hay-
Broken Hill track. Then after turning right towards Hay, the
road would branch in a south-western direction and head
towards Echuca. This was the way the others had explained
their movements. It was hard for Joe to estimate his speed,
for now with half his team he could only guess that he was
doing half the full team's speed. He decided he was doing
better than that and that by nightfall he would be eight to
ten miles further along.

Later, as the sun set behind him, Joe had not come to
the crossing. Ahead lay endless plains, the claypans glowing
red as the late sun shimmered across them. There was no
sign of a tree line indicating the chance of a waterhole.
Eventually he made camp, deciding it best to rest the bullocks, so that at first light they could start off in search of
water in the cool of the day.

During the night Joe thought about the future of his
three remaining bullocks. The cargo of wool would miss the

sales, but its value would remain. Through fits of restless sleep Joe decided that if he came to a station property he would abandon this trip, sell the bullocks, ask that the wool be stored, and get a message about his predicament to the owner of the wool.

Two hours after his five o'clock start Joe came to a cross-track. Instinctively he turned to the west, for he had travelled in a south-easterly direction for some days now. By heading west he would at least be trapped by river systems, even though he had no idea how distant they might be. His animals by now were visibly deteriorating. Experience told him that once the flanks of the bullock fell away so too did their working ability. Again he was forced to change his plan. He would travel by night, for the moon would be full for the next couple of nights and in that half-light they could travel more easily out of the sun. He could only hope his mates were behind him, for if they were in front they would be moving ahead, leaving him behind.

After two more days Joe had still not found water. Some clusters of trees had offered hope, only to be dashed on closer inspection where the cracked pattern of dry mud greeted him like some evil web.

Ten days after he had departed on his return trip he saw in the distance a shimmering haze. He cursed it, for this time he would not be fooled by another mirage. He continued in the same direction but continued to look back, noticing that the changed angle from the sun's glare did not seem to change the distant object as it should have. Reluctantly he turned the team in its direction. Soon the shimmering stopped and the roofline of a station property stood welcoming against the never-ending backdrop.

The station owner was a predictable type. Generally they seemed the same, leaner than the more prosperous southern pastoralists. They lived more by their instincts and skills, tested always by their isolation.

Matt Brewer was such a man, and as he considered Joe's plight there was no indication of inconvenience. For Matt it was a problem to be solved. As it happened, he too had a loaded wagon of wool and was set to leave for Echuca in the morning. Matt was a horse man. His team of eight would pull a little less than Joe's three bullocks had been hauling. He had thirty horses, for they were his love, and regular sales of trained harness horses gave him an extra income.

An hour went by as Matt inspected the wagon and particularly the harness. Several times he pushed his hat back on his head as he peered up at the loaded wagon, then looking down, his hand still at the edge of his hat, his fingers would scratch at his forehead before the adjustment was made.

Invited into the homestead, Joe was offered a cup of tea. Typically, the kitchen was the living area. A large wood stove at one end identified the engine of the room, for steam spurted and faded as a saucepan rocked gently on its hotplate, belching out a build-up of vapour. Joe and Matt sat around the table, while Matt's wife busily cut into potatoes at another.

Matt lifted a mug of tea, about to drink, then replacing it on the table he thought for a moment. He had ten good horses, he explained to Joe, that he'd planned to sell at the Echuca horse sales next month. If he could adapt the bullock harness to suit the horses it would be a way of getting his horses to market and Joe's wool to its destination.

'It would save me another trip down later, if they came with us. I don't see why we couldn't change the harness to suit them. They'd lose some condition, but a month's spell before the sales would bring 'em back to top. The teamwork would do 'em good too. They'd be a neat team by the time we got there.'

Joe couldn't believe his good luck. He started to mutter some words of thanks, but was cut short. 'Now give those bullocks some feed, they'll have to follow behind.' It was obvious that in Matt's eyes the bullock was an inferior beast to the horse. 'I'll start getting that harness adjusted.'

The next day two wagons headed off across the plains. The fresh horses would make good time, their jerky motion heralding an urgency to the task, so different from the slow pull and sway of the bullocks, which trailed behind, tethered to the wagon. Joe wondered if they knew they were now a liability.

They reached Echuca in four days, and at the wharf where hundreds of bales stood waiting for loading Joe caught up with Clarrie and Ben, who had arrived two days earlier. The date was September the second, and as arranged in the contracts, Clarrie and Ben would make their £90, and refund of deposit, though they had missed the bonus set for an August fifteen delivery. There was also the loss of a bullock each. The two had not forgotten the action of the Aborigines. It became their talking point around the wharf by day, and in the pubs by night.

Joe was relieved to have finally checked his cargo onto the steamer *Angora*, pleased that the disaster was at least finished with. He counted the cost. He had lost his deposit, there was no payment due, and he had lost three of his bullocks. From the £340 and his team of six he had lost £100 deposit, and half his team at £60. That left Joe with £180 after his twelve months on the road. It would not be enough for the hardware store. It was to have been his last chance, and it had failed. The thought of again returning to his brother's foundry weighed on Joe, for he was no longer a young man. He would from tomorrow be in his fiftieth year.

Tomorrow he would make that decision. Tonight he

would sit with the other teamsters and share the stories of those good times 'bullocking up north', for it would be the last time.

Joe remained in Echuca for a month after the wool was disposed of. Matt had business in Melbourne, but had trouble agisting the horses in the town or its outskirts. In gratitude Joe offered to care for the horses, and together they mapped out a plan to feed and exercise them while he was away so that they would be in top condition on his return just before the sales.

There was another reason. Joe needed time to plan his immediate future. Though now too old for foundry work, he was not too old to complete all that writing, to find a way of putting it together as the so-called experts had advised. For now he was ready to accept others' advice, to cut into his writings, to tear away at the jumble of words so that all the tales, all the bits of stories could be made into one. Gone would be the phrases that rebounded on the previous sentence, hindering the flow; in their place would be some straight wording that took the characters down a predictable path.

This was not his way but what others had demanded. Joe had written a long letter to Kate and given it to Matt, who promised to deliver it on his arrival in Melbourne. In it he expressed his desire to co-operate with the publishers; with her help they would rework and reword, till the publishers were content and his work finally printed. He told her of his disastrous final trip, mentioning the financial loss, but mostly he talked of his feeling towards her. They were not the usual words of love, not strong or masculine, or rushed with urgent demands, but rather subtly tender, caressing her at the edges of reason, a gentle teasing.

He had also got word to Leonie and the boys, explaining that he had money to bring home, but not as much as he had hoped for. He had sent £60 home via the bank. He would have £200 to go home with. He told them how he had missed them all. And it was true, for there were still glowing coals beneath the extinguished flames of his marriage, when a man's sense of duty towards his family pulled at his conscience, forging a coupling that would withstand the separations of time and interest.

The days went quickly, for his attendance on the horses was required early morning and late afternoon. The rest of his day was given to writing by hand passages that might fit into those places where the critics had wanted cuts. He must add a directness that would give his story a plausible narrative line. As he had explained to Kate, 'I find this job too much like pulling down a house and building a skillion.'

When Matt returned one week before the sales, Joe wished him farewell, adding that he should get top price for his horses, for he had made it known to the locals that this was the team that pulled a wagon stacked with bales that were too much for a bullock team. And when Joe moved on down the road, heading south, he knew he would never be northward bound again.

CHAPTER 19

The
Rivals

SAM, FELIX AND Ted had made good progress. Ted's father-in-law, who owned the shed from which they now operated, had helped with some capital. They had made all the moulding boxes and finished the tank end pattern. There was much discussion on what words and what style of lettering they should put. It was here that Ted showed his entrepreneurial skills, suggesting they should keep it simple, such as, 'Furphy Bros Water Tank', with the option that the name could be changed if they supplied the end only to other potential makers of the water cart.

The only problem that remained was that of the supply of sand. John Furphy had arranged delivery of his sand from Melbourne, where it was taken from the marshy beach areas of Frankston and Oakleigh. It was the only supply, and they were unable to buy from the supplier, who had suggested there was enough foundry production in the area. They all wondered if there was some collusion between the parties. Unfussed, Ted again showed his initiative when he experimented with local sands. The early moulds were too rough, the sand too coarse until he added a fine clay dust that made a pliable material with a smooth texture.

The date was set for Wednesday the eighth of September 1891 for the start of production. The new foundry looked neat, boxes all stacked in an orderly manner, sand heaped in rows. With its addition of clay, the sand held an inner strength it would need to withstand the constant battering of the rammer, the sharp wash of molten metal. It was a kind of miracle that each grain kept its shape after this continuous assault. As is the way with foundries, the boys knew it would never look so neat again.

John was now fully aware of his nephews' program. The meeting with Maisie had had one good outcome, for he had redeemed himself, overcome the temptations of the flesh and somehow thrown his lustful actions back onto Maisie. But the information she had given him was of little use. There was nothing there he did not know already, so he had reluctantly accepted that there was little chance of him stopping the Mooroopna foundry. Wal Gregory, Ted's father-in-law, was a man of some substance, and as the local butcher was well known in that area west of the river, the same place John had passed through fifteen years ago and very nearly settled at.

John decided that he would go ahead with getting a patent on the water cart. Realising that it would require much red tape, he decided to engage a law firm in Melbourne who would expedite the application. Even a notice of his intention might be sufficient to delay the production of another brand of water cart—a notice threatening in its form, with ample legal jargon to confuse those Furphy traitors and mixed with straight talk that would spell out the serious implications for those who poached the works of others.

The only worthwhile news from Maisie was of Joe's

whereabouts. She had told him that Joe had had trouble up north, that he was now on his way home and that he had finished with bullock-driving. John decided he would wait for Joe's return. Better that the legal document be handed to him than to those sons of his who were likely to discard it, not caring about the consequences. At least he could still talk to his brother.

William was told of his father's plan. He quickly agreed, suggesting that he add the words 'Patent Pending' to the tank end. This was a common mark on quality British machinery that somehow added to its status, simple but daunting, giving an air of British justice and authority.

CHAPTER 20

Joe's
Return

LONG AGO PEOPLE had told Leonie that she was like a butterfly, and she liked to think of this as meaning not that she flitted from one thing to another but that her lightness of touch brought a gracefulness pleasing in the sight of others. In her teenage years when she helped her mother at the hotel she would glide efficiently from one chore to another, the light touch of hands expertly working—glasses filled, a swipe of the bar with a clean cloth so that reflections showed of gnarled old hands with a glass in between, the patrons' hands resting easy, hers quick and white, the servants of others.

Now Leonie pondered the fit of the image, for somehow the butterfly had not developed fully, but had rather reverted to the lumbering crawl of the caterpillar it once was. Now more than ever she longed for a return to that clear lightness of efficiency, for she saw her sons filled with new purpose, eating like horses, the new work exhausting them physically but not sapping their energy. Late at night after supper she would watch them in discussion, their eyes alight

147

with plans and figures, their limbs reclined at youthful angles into uncomfortable chairs. As never before, she could see that they were happy, and she longed to join them. If only the box of her soured marriage could break open and release her into something—anything, but something other than the dragging confinement she knew each day.

Then one day Joe returned. He was suddenly there on the doorstep, his familiar worn face shaded by his old hat. She tried to fly to him, but found herself held back, moving to greet him but then retracting, like a puppet butterfly on a string. And like trapped wings fluttering against the net, her conscience pulled in all directions.

Joe, too, was hesitant as he clasped his wife's shoulders, for they were strangers. It took time for them to thaw, to take on again some semblance of real people. Joe saw the tiredness in her eyes, a distress he could only guess at, and a new pity took hold of him. His roving life was over, and here was this wife he did not love but knew he had to be with to the end of his days. Here were his boys also, already launched on a new life, asking him to work with them. There was a relief in just being part of a family, wherever his affections lay.

They talked into the night. Sam and Felix related the whole story, how William had lied, blaming them for casting rejects, how their uncle John had made impossible demands for them to increase production, and finally their plan and eventual realisation of a longtime dream.

Joe told his stories from up north: the drought, the Aborigines, the disaster at the waterhole, the combination of bad luck and mismanagement that had taken most of his savings over that long year. And before they went to bed there was another cup of coffee from Leonie, now at ease moving between the chairs and the stove. Then Sam, in a changed voice, a voice of authority, a man's voice, said:

'It'll be good to have you with us, Dad. At the moment we're busy. I mentioned it to Ted and he suggested you could do deliveries and pick-ups. That way you can work your own hours.'

Joe thought about it for a long time that night. It was perfect. Some small income, time out to write, and trips to Melbourne. But best of all, freedom from a dependence on his brother. Leonie sighed in the bed nearby. They both rolled into sleep facing the nearest wall.

CHAPTER 21

Brothers in Contest

THE RIVALRY BETWEEN foundries was put aside momentarily over an incident that as it turned out was close to the hearts of both Joe and John.

Before Joe left on his last trip up north, he had helped to form a literary guild in Shepparton. He had accepted a position on its committee, even though, as he had explained, he would be away for at least twelve months. The others had insisted he be on the foundation committee, for they were well aware of his literary talent. The committee had worked well, receiving funds to purchase land on which they had a temporary iron shed. It was the beginnings of the town's Mechanics' Institute and Library.

John had also been part of this guild, though not yet on its committee. The elder brother was gifted in his own way with words. The imaginative side of his practical life had flowed in different directions from Joe's: into the rousing eloquence of the lay preacher inveighing against the evils of society—substantial, useful stuff, as he saw it, not the vapourings of irresponsible bushmen that Joe seemed to favour. As children the brothers had respected each other's skill at writing and speaking, but they had also had a secret rivalry over their gift with words.

Beside his sermons, John was the author of several tracts and a well-known essay on Federation that had been published in the *Bulletin*. He had continued to attend the guild's meetings while Joe was away, and had cast envious eyes at the committee. He knew elections were at hand. This was the time to assert himself over the ridiculous reputation his brother had acquired over some silly stories and verses in the *Bulletin*.

On the second night after his return, Joe received a notice of the monthly meeting, at which a new committee was to be elected. He looked forward to renewing acquaintances, for these were his closest friends in Shepparton. For his own purposes, he knew that this establishment would become his home away from home, as the Institute in Kyneton had been, for already there was a good range of material stored: manuscripts, local government minutes, issues of the *Bulletin* and the colonies' various newspapers. One item he had found puzzling was a series of fifteen handwritten sermons displayed in a wooden frame along one wall. The writing was familiar. They were his brother's sermons, each with their curious names: 'Harvest', 'Embrace', 'Sunshine'. Tess and Dulcie Douglas, Don's sisters, would have been responsible for having them framed and hung, for they were devout Methodists as well as keen members of the guild. But Joe wondered if it was their idea alone.

The committee had determined that Joe Furphy should be elected chairman now that he had returned. Dulcie and Tess, who were besotted with John, their preacher, who provided work for their brother and therefore a livelihood for them, had mistakenly thought the committee, of which they were members, were referring to John rather than Joe. It was never determined just how the mistake was made—perhaps because someone had carelessly written just 'J. Furphy' in the minutes and the sisters had assumed that their esteemed preacher was meant. At any rate Dulcie had told John privately at a lunch meeting how happy she was that the committee was nominating him for chairman.

The meeting was about to commence when John walked in. He had timed his entrance to maximise his presence, for this was a night that would bring him another position of office in Shepparton. It was the part of meetings he enjoyed, the anticipation of things delayed, the heightened expectation that his importance would be recognised.

William Montgomery was a large man, ideal for opening a meeting, for as always there was need to silence the eighteen or so members who talked loudly among themselves. He rose and called for order, declaring the meeting open before John had found himself a seat, much to John's annoyance, for all turned to the chairman and his entry was spoiled. When John finally found a seat he did as some of his congregation did when late and trying not to be noticed—slid with an undignified sideways movement onto the chair.

After a brief summary of the year's activity, Montgomery handed over to the acting secretary-treasurer. As with other office-bearers, all positions had been temporary for that first year. Tonight would see the right people in the right places. The formalities over, Montgomery declared that the next item on the agenda was the election of office-bearers. He was about to call for nominations when John rose. The clatter he made with his chair was deliberate, like the drum roll announcing the trapeze artist.

'Mr Chairman,' he began. 'On behalf of those present I'm sure that it's time to formally to thank yourself, the Secretary-Treasurer and Committee for your dedicated work on this interim Committee. An important aspect of this young town's fabric is the participation of people in cultural activity. We have all heard, indeed you have reiterated, Mr Chairman, that Government assistance is available to those who are organised and look to the future. I am confident that through your good work we will soon have what all towns dream of, a Mechanics' Institute and Library.'

John then moved a motion that recorded their efforts, and as mover was well aware that his name would also be recorded. But more than that, for he had set firmly in the minutes a precedent for others to follow at subsequent annual meetings. Similar words would surely be said of him one year from now. As he sat, his eyes scanned the audience, something he was practised at from the pulpit.

It was then that he saw, with consternation, that his brother Joe was there, seated at the back of the hall. He was unaware that he had returned. He began to feel uneasy, for he knew the high regard most of the guild had for Joe's writing, and he wondered why they would not have nominated him for chairman. And yet Dulcie had told him that he, John, was their prearranged nomination. Inwardly he cursed his brother—could they not keep out of each other's path? And now there was the possibility of a public contest between them. He might have known to look at the back of the hall, for Joe always took his place behind people—he had no dignity, John thought with annoyance, no sense of occasion. It occurred to him that it was where Joe would sit when around a camp fire.

John did not wish to humiliate Joe publicly, as he knew would happen if it came to a vote between them, and he was relieved when he remembered that he would have a chance, in a short while after he was elected, to refer to Joe's good work for the guild. And as chairman he would have a legitimate power over Joe, for Joe was a mere hand in his foundry, apart from his writings a man of no consequence in the town. His train of thought went to the rival foundry and his recent humiliation at Leonie's door, and he started to fume, but decided to put the matter from his mind until later. He had that sort of discipline, he thought. That was why he had got on in the world.

Montgomery was on his feet again, his stomach extended over the table top. 'It's now time,' he began, 'for the election of office-bearers, and as I am just an interim chairman I can only conduct the election of the new chairman, after which he will take over and conduct the remaining elections for the evening. Now if you're all in agreement'—he did not wait for objections—'I hereby call for nominations for the position of Chairman of the Shepparton Literary Guild.'

Dulcie Douglas was on her feet before he had finished. Montgomery was looking at Edward Rowlands, who was now just rising to his feet. He was moving slowly, for he was savouring the importance of his nomination of Joe, expecting that, as planned, this would be the only one.

But Dulcie was speaking: 'Mr Chairman, I wish to nominate John Furphy. He's a leading citizen, and ...'

Montgomery interrupted. 'There'll be no speaking to the nomination. Now would you repeat your nomination?' He was sure she had mentioned John's name mistakenly and meant it to be Joe. After all she and her sister knew the arrangement.

'I would like to nominate John Furphy.' Dulcie's voice was raised now and quite clear. Montgomery hesitated, unsure. He knew he must except the nomination, but decided to try and delay its acceptance.

'Thank you, Dulcie. Now I'll just call for other nominations.' He looked at Rowlands and nodded, for the man seemed confused. 'Edward Rowlands, you have a nomination?' Montgomery lowered his voice, realising he was putting words into his mouth. After a silence he said: 'Yes, Mr

Chairman, I wish to nominate Joseph Furphy as Chairman.'

'Good, thank you.' Montgomery raised his voice a notch. 'So I have a nomination for Joseph Furphy.' He hesitated, hoping that Dulcie would realise her mistake. 'Now, Dulcie Douglas, do you wish to continue with your nomination?' She was not at all flustered, he noticed. She rose quickly, and said, with a hint of anger, 'Yes, Mr Chairman, I've said it twice before.' If she had made a mistake she was not going to back down now, and besides, her sister was still prompting her.

The two nominations were accepted. John wondered if he should accept. He was experienced with meetings and was aware that positions were often prearranged. Rowlands and Montgomery had made it clear that Joe's nomination was the planned one. What did that damned woman mean by telling him he was to be nominated? He reassured himself that in any vote he would certainly win, for Montgomery and Rowlands would surely support their preacher, even if the latter had nominated someone else; Montgomery was the choirmaster, and Rowlands treasurer of the church funds. He could not bring himself to decline the nomination.

Knowing how his brother hated airing family matters in public, Joe wondered if John would withdraw and refuse his nomination. Rivals or not, there had always been a clear demarcation of their individual expertise, and he knew he had pre-eminence over John as a writer and felt certain the guild would elect him. Furthermore, he sometimes wondered if John did not despise these people, for he had referred to some of them as social layabouts and do-gooders.

But there was no move from John, and now Montgomery was announcing: 'One speaker for each nomination, to be followed by a vote.' Hesitating, he followed with the form of vote: 'A show of hands.' He would have preferred a secret ballot but was not confident it could be arranged.

Dulcie was quick to respond. She had prepared a list of John's past, present, and continuing achievements. It was rehearsed, couched in phrases of adoration. She finished with: 'What man do you know of who is a major employer, on at least three major committees, yet finds time for his maker, and helps us all to praise God's glory?' She seemed to sit down several times and stand again, as if loath to relinquish her precious public moment. The women present assumed she was rearranging her several layers of petticoats.

Montgomery turned to Edward Rowlands, who by now was pink with embarrassment, totally flustered by having his preacher stand against the man he had nominated. He had not expected to have to speak, and speaking in public was something he had never done. Now, not only did he have to speak before a gathering of people but he had a duty to at least match the previous speaker. His mind, usually sharp with figures, laboured as if a fog had rolled in. He struggled to find words, then decided to get it over with quickly. 'Joe would make a good Chairman,' he said lamely. His voice trailed off and he sat down quickly.

Montgomery was wanting to move on. 'Well, we've heard about the two candidates, both worthy of leading us into the future.' There was a shifting of chairs and he could sense an unease in the hall. 'Now voting will be by a show of hands, but I'm asking that Joe and John step outside while we conduct the vote.' Joe moved to the door quickly, for he also wished this whole episode over. John remained seated, reluctant, for he could see a vote or two going Joe's way with him out of the room. Then slowly he went to the door, his demeanour threatening those unsure of their vote.

Montgomery continued, 'All those in favour of John Furphy as Chairman, please raise your right hand.'

He counted quickly, then, wondering if he'd made a mistake, counted again more slowly. There were two groups seated on separate sides of the hall: Dulcie, her sister, and one other, and on the other side four men, two of whom worked with John, the other two on his Water Trust Board. Then there was one vote in the middle. Montgomery was not surprised that Edward Rowlands had his hand up for John. That made eight.

'Now those in favour of Joseph Furphy as Chairman.' His voice faltered as he realised that his vote and subsequent casting vote would see Joe elected. The whole embarrassing evening was his to decide.

Seven hands went up, hesitantly, not wanting to be first to declare, then more quickly. Montgomery's raised hand sealed the vote as a draw.

'Eight votes each', he declared. 'As Chairman conducting this election, I give my casting vote to Joe.' He wanted it known loud and clear, for he knew what others at the meeting did not. Over recent weeks Maisie Sheppard had confided in Montgomery after choir practice. She had told him of John's lustful fondling of her, and the way she described it both disgusted and excited him, for he also had had certain fantasies about Maisie. But to go so far as to actually ... Words failed him.

Outside, Joe had moved down the hall building to an alcove, where he relit his pipe, sheltered from the wind. He started to count the votes of those inside, but soon gave up, realising that he had lost contact with these people over the last year, to the point where he could not be sure of John's influence over them. He would have liked to be chairman, but he would not have sought this distasteful contest.

When John left the hall he immediately caught the pungent aroma drifting downwind. Tonight was not the night to approach his brother. He moved a few steps from the door in the opposite direction. He remembered how in their youth they shared things, gave in to each other when necessary. For a moment he regretted that it had come to this, but soon he too was counting those he could rely on. He decided he would have the numbers, but that it would be close.

There was a whispered call asking for their return to the meeting. John was not so sure of himself now. There were no faces looking up at him as he strode to his seat, reassuring himself that every one was just a little embarrassed with the two brothers running. He directed his attention to Montgomery. There was no apparent unease there. Surely if he had lost, Montgomery would be a little nervous.

Joe sat easy. He had resigned himself to losing. He would make a point of congratulating his brother before the night was over.

The announcement was made quickly, and the silence that followed accentuated Montgomery's heavy footstep as he strode down the hall to where Joe sat, then extended his hand. He, at least, was pleased with the result.

Joe was standing now, the pipe at the side of his mouth. That, and the unfolding smile, gave him an engaging larrikin look. Increasingly now others moved up to congratulate him. He forgot John in his simple happiness at having his writer friends around him, applauding. Some of his locked inhibitions released themselves, so that a Joe he had forgotten existed brimmed from the light-hearted romantic who now walked to the front of the hall. He sat in the chair Montgomery had vacated. He had been to enough meetings to know the procedure. Thanking members for their support, he moved straight on with the election of office-bearers then closed the meeting.

The Douglas sisters had been muttering to each other in a corner. The supper, which they usually served with cheerful energy, went on as if in slow motion, the sisters' eyes directed only to the task at hand, for only now had they realised their mistake. They had tried to convey their apologies to John, who said nothing except to excuse himself from their presence. Going over to Montgomery, John indicated his embarrassment, adding with tight lips that this unnecessary farce would spoil the start of the Society's year.

Joe was working his way to John. Others were pressing around him. When next he looked, his brother was gone.

CHAPTER 22

Legal
Action

IN THE WEEKS that passed Joe had all but forgotten his brother and his foundry. His days were full: time to work his own hours with his sons, time to work on matters to do with the literary guild, and more time than ever before to write and rewrite, which would soon lead to his pilgrimage to Melbourne.

John had kept a low profile in those weeks, his mind in continual judgment of those that voted on that night, and now not confident that those he had thought revered him would not have voted against him. He had considered them one by one, and each time he did so the names changed places, until they became like so many penned sheep, turning in circles, perplexed, straining to move in any direction.

He had not been able to bring himself to track Joe down. Instead he had instructed his solicitors to serve notice on Joe, his sons, and young Ted Newby. The notice was in front of him now and he liked the way it read—very much to the point, couched in strong words that conjured up a severity that could not be ignored.

Dear Sir,

Our client John Furphy has informed us of your intention to manufacture a type of Water Cart based on the product made by my client. Please be aware that any attempt by you to copy the design of the Water Cart is quite improper and my client intends to take whatever steps necessary to prevent you from carrying out your intentions. Please be hereby notified that a formal application for a Patent has been lodged with the Patents Office that will protect my client's rights over the manufacture of the Water Cart.

It is therefore strongly suggested that you desist from your plans, and we give notice that we are instructed to take whatever legal steps are necessary to prevent you from going any further with production of the Water Cart.

The drought of 1893 was now more severe than the nuisance dry spells of '91 and '92, to the extent that the farmers and local communities were no longer purchasing goods, but where possible, as their forefathers had often done in Ireland, they improvised, rationed and scaled back to more humble necessities. Towards the end of 1893 businesses, shops and factories were forced to close down. Australia was in the midst of its first depression.

For John and his establishment, the drought at first had the effect of boom times as farmers purchased the water cart to distribute a precious commodity. But drought had started the depression, and soon the farmers had resorted to wooden barrels and kerosene tins as containers. John's sales had dropped, but the wealthy pastoralists somehow seemed able to call on extra funds to purchase necessities and Furphy's water cart was considered one of these.

Felix, Sam and Ted were also losing out. Their sales of water carts had also dropped badly and they had not had time to bring on other product lines as planned. All this, however, was not of as much concern as the document received from the Shepparton lawyer. There were no other lawyers in the district from whom to seek a quick opinion of their rights, so Joe offered to take the letter to Melbourne with him next week to check the ramifications. As it turned out, Kate mixed with some leading Melbourne solicitors and he was sure she might help him here.

CHAPTER 23

Kate and Melbourne

IN MELBOURNE JOE saw contradictory signs of poverty and prosperity. He saw queues of unemployed and undernourished children clad in rags, but on the streets and on corner blocks there seemed to be a minor building boom. Kate explained to him that the wealthy were now even richer than on his last visit over a year ago, for although the gold was beginning to dwindle for many prospectors, established mining companies were still reaping huge rewards and were spending their wealth on grand hotels, shops and palatial homes.

Kate had left her parents' home and had taken rooms in the centre of town with Delia Crossby, a fellow librarian. As Joe knocked on the heavy oak door he wondered if city life might have changed Kate's attitude to a country friend. He was reassured when the door opened and Kate rushed to him, flinging her arms round his neck in an impetuous embrace.

In the hours that followed they swamped each other with question and answer, racing, then hesitant, until, late

165

into the night, exhausted conversation gave way to silence. She had made up a bed for him in the spare room. It was a token gesture towards correctness, for Joe used the bed only half the night. Delia, it appeared, was conveniently out of town for a few days.

The next day Kate donned her schoolmarm correctness again. Her dark hair, which had flowed around him in the night, was pinned back primly. They told each other much of their literary progress over the last year, and determined that together they would solve the problem of Joe's proliferation of words that others, according to the critics, would not read.

Joe was surprised at the extent of editing she had done on *Such Is Life*. Whole passages were missing, yet she was able to show that the shorter version still contained a meandering flow that was true to his style. The two days that followed were crowded in blissful unison, Joe more often than before agreeing to her suggestions and allowing a subtle rearrangement. He was pleased that his recent writings in Echuca were useful, appreciative that Kate was able to slide a new passage into a section of text as if she had instructed him to write the material through mental telepathy.

By the time Kate had finished this editing, it was the equivalent of writing her own novel. She had decided that she would not tell Joe she had worked an average of three hours a day on most days over that last year. Over that same year she had sought advice from connections of Joe's. They were aware of her obsession with Joe's work and often hesitant to co-operate with her, fearing she was too close to those that would eventually make the decision to publish.

Joe too was aware by now of Kate's faith in his work. He wondered if he should offer her some financial reward if ever it was published. And if it failed, well, he would reward her now, by taking her to what was considered the finest eatery in Melbourne, Pellegrini's.

The moon was full on that spring night as they walked from her rooms to the restaurant. Still low in the sky, its orange light lit the edges of buildings and reached into the streets and lanes. Their window table overlooked a crowded street. Kate seemed unconcerned about the queues that waited on the opposite side for a meal dished out from a soup kitchen. Joe had not seen such poverty before; depression always showed in the cities first. But he ate the rather elaborate meal without comment, not wishing to spoil the evening for Kate.

Later, over coffee, Joe explained his need to seek legal advice and asked Kate if she knew anyone in the legal fraternity who might help. He had only tomorrow left in Melbourne and he knew he must set it aside on his other great challenge.

Stark & Willman, Solicitors, were located in the heart of the legal strip, an Australian copy of London's Gray's Inn. The buildings identified their occupants as members of the wealthy classes. Kate had dealt with Stark on several related matters to do with the fledgling education system, for which there seemed no end of change. She had moved from teaching some years back and now with a group of ex-teachers and some bureaucrats was responsible for putting into practice the ever-changing policies of the government.

Stark was good at his work, but often told Kate of his longing for a change to something more challenging, like court work. The table that separated Joe and the lawyer was huge, and so when Joe began his explanation for his visit he found himself leaning forward, arms folded on the table, so that Stark might hear him without raising his voice. He told of his brother's and sons' conflicting businesses. Then, reading the letter from John's solicitors, he noticed a faint spark of enthusiasm crinkle from the edge of Stark's eye. It was a slight matter that Stark knew he should not contemplate further, but Kate had mentioned that Joe was the writer 'Warrigal Jack'.

The lawyer found himself looking at a man he would have travelled miles to meet, fascinated that this lean old bushman was much as he had imagined the *Bulletin's* 'Warrigal Jack' to be. He understood for the first time why a man capable of such writing could humble himself by hiding his real name under a pseudonym: there was no more pretension in his heart than fat on his body.

As he warmed to the man, Stark decided he would take up this matter. He might be able to repay Furphy for the pages of verse and prose that had given him such pleasure, by writing, in the legal jargon Joe could never have mastered, a document that would not only favour his honoured client but also have the effect of satisfying his need for more challenging work.

He began by asking Joe about the workings and the products of the two foundries, about the water cart and its function, trying to draw from Joe a way around what looked like an impossible task, particularly where patents were concerned. Joe mentioned the tank end casting component and how others would also make the tank if they could manufacture the casting. Stark asked if the end was the main component and if so what value it had to the completed tank.

'At least half,' Joe said. 'You see, any blacksmith or wheelwright can roll up a cylinder, and hand-forge an expansion hoop. But the ends can't be forged. Steel plate would require a thickness that would make the tank too heavy.'

He thought for a while, then suggested that Joe leave for an hour or two so that he could work on a response that might allow for a negotiated settlement. For that was all he could hope for.

This suited Joe as he had arranged to meet Kate for

lunch. They sat in a small café in the vicinity of Princes Bridge. Kate was excited, for she had received a letter from A.G. Stephens, editor of the *Bulletin*, who had asked when her next revision of *Such Is Life* would be sent. He also said that he had lost contact with Joe, explaining that he might soon need to negotiate if publication was to go ahead.

They walked back to Kate's office, in and out of warm sun as they glided under shady trees, winding their arms around each other tighter as if the book were binding them together. Joe forced away any pangs of guilt at being with this young woman, for the city was big and busy now and swallowed them in its anonymity. Tomorrow they would be on their separate paths, like driftwood, Joe thought, floating downstream until pulled to the backwater of deep and slow consideration, then swirling together in a whirlpool of emotion.

At the solicitor's Joe did not need to see Stark again. A large envelope was simply handed to him by the receptionist. The journey home went quickly for Joe. He had read the contents of the envelope and marvelled at the simplicity of the lawyer's solution to the problem. It began with the advice that they would be very unwise to continue to manufacture the water cart. He had checked at the Patents Office and found that an application had indeed been lodged. He explained a possible way round the difficulty: manufacturing the ends only with a view to selling them to others who might or might not be in breach of the patent, depending on the area of assembly. Joe warmed to the idea, for he knew his sons had often talked of other blacksmiths and wheelwrights who had requested ends only with a view to making their own cart.

CHAPTER 24

Sweet
Victory

BACK AT MOOROOPNA, the drought
that continued across the nation had taken effect. Farms had
ceased to produce, and their owners' buying was reduced to
zero. The foundry operated at less than half-pace. Joe could
detect a lack of momentum that would drag on the workmen's day, for he had a theory that in foundries, the slower
the workload, the more the labour became an ordeal and the
more the workmen's spirits became depressed.

John's foundry had reduced its work force by half, and
over the river Joe's boys and Ted were down to just themselves and one other. It was not the ideal time to approach
potential makers of water carts. On the other hand, they had
little else to do. They worked in pairs: Felix and his father
then Sam and Ted, each spending a portion of their working
week visiting those on a predetermined list with a blacksmithing capacity.

After two weeks they estimated there were four defi-
nite manufacturers with a combined sales estimate of ten
tanks per week. There were others whose marketing and

manufacturing capacity it was harder to assess. To be safe they put a figure on them of three tanks in total. This came to thirteen tanks per week, just eight short of their budgeted amount. But it was enough for Joe to instruct Starks to prepare a letter that would counter the action proposed by his brother.

The letter stated in the usual legal jargon that the Furphy Bros Foundry in Mooroopna would cease production of the water cart at the end of the year, two months away, explaining that this time was required to honour outstanding orders, many of which were in the process of a form of time payment. There was little else explained. John and his sons, having gone over the letter several times, were satisfied, for not only had they successfully shielded their water cart from their predatory relatives, but this also would surely lead to the closing of the rival foundry. The two-month delay was of little consequence, for it was unlikely that the drought would break now, given that the summer season was about to commence.

Two weeks before Christmas, however, the Furphy Bros Foundry was still producing tank ends. John and William had spied on the works regularly, and wondered why, if they were ceasing production in two weeks, they would be stockpiling ends.

The Christmas–New Year break saw the local industry shut down for a period. John and his family had reason to celebrate, for now, as before, they would run the only foundry in the area.

But two weeks later both foundries were open for business again and the two spies again noticed that the production of tank ends was still in progress at Mooroopna. This indicated to them that the production of water carts must be continuing.

John could not contain his anxiety any longer and decided to present himself to Joe and his sons, with the letter from his lawyer. He arranged for a meeting at Joe's house on the next night. He was surprised that Joe had agreed to the meeting, particularly at his house, for he was not in the habit of visiting Joe, and Leonie must have told him of his last humiliating appearance.

The next night John, William and George followed, single file, up the narrow path. At the front door John did the knocking. The knock needed to indicate confidence, and it did: three knocks strong and clear, followed by two even louder. George cringed a little. It was the part of his father he did not like.

Joe was prepared, for he knew full well the purpose of the visit and tonight, just maybe tonight, he would silence his brother with a twist he could not argue with.

Leonie answered the door. She did not leave the kitchen-cum-dining room where the meeting was to take place. She would make her presence felt, even if it was as someone not bothered with the importance of his business. Age had not been unkind to her, for although her body had rounded, her face still showed an alert countenance, the sharp but petite features still tomboyish as she was when Joe first mistook her for a teenage boy. Her hair, now pulled back in a bun, revealed the firm, youthful skin of her face and neck.

She noticed with pleasure that George called her Auntie Leonie. He was the one she liked most, for he and Charles were well liked by their cousins. It had often been the subject of discussion at Joe's house. They hoped that one day these young men would break the shackles that held them to their father and older brother.

The kitchen had a large table at one end; there were six chairs. Joe, Sam and Felix stood at the places they normally sat at. There was limited greeting, the tone of the meeting already strictly formal.

Joe began with something of an understatement. 'Well John, I believe you have something to talk about.' Leonie had placed herself at the stove, for this was her area of command and she would reassert her claim by checking the oven every so often.

John unfolded the original letter that had been sent to Joe. 'Joe, your time has expired,' he said, stabbing at the paper with a forefinger. 'We felt generous enough in allowing you to continue the manufacture of our water cart till Christmas. Well, it's past that now, and if you don't cease forthwith, I feel I should warn you that my solicitor will be informing the police, who may make arrests.' He added, 'I have checked with the local constabulary and they are prepared to carry out the law, Joe.'

William stood quickly, for like his father, his presence was all-important. 'We have a patent in place, and you are breaking it. It is a law of the Crown and carries a gaol term if broken.'

Sam didn't stand, just moved his huge arms off the table, leaning back to expose a broad chest and neck that showed vertical ripples of sinew and vein under smooth brown skin. 'But we ain't doing nothing wrong, just hard working, as we did for yous, once.' His voice matched his demeanour. The words were powerful without being shouted.

'A bullock can work too, but it's got no brains.' William was standing again, his voice becoming shrill, but he was cut short as his father's large hand pulled him down onto the chair again. His father was better practised at controlling this sort of situation.

John continued. 'But we know you're still making them. It's been witnessed by others and recorded.'

Joe broke in. 'What's been recorded?'

John was losing patience. 'You are still making it ... the

174

water cart. You're still making the water cart.' He slowed the words, so that they might sink in to slow minds.

Joe broke in again. 'But we're not making them.'

'We've seen with our own eyes.' John did not want to admit to spying, but they had to be convinced that it was no good hiding the truth.

'What 'ave ya seen?' Sam joined in.

'You continue to produce the tank end for your water cart.' Again John spelt it out slowly. There was a long pause. Were they so slow of wit that they did not understand, or were they so guilty that they could not speak?

With a voice as calm as his brother's, Joe slowly delivered his trump card. 'We make the end, John, yes, but it's not for our water cart. It's for others, and I have a legal opinion from a Melbourne lawyer that what we do now is quite within the law. What is it we're making a week, boys?'

'Thirty-six ends.' Felix had the figures at his fingertips. 'That's as many as you were making, or do you make that number now, Uncle John?' There was an edge of guilt to his voice, for Felix had been told by Joe to exaggerate the figure a little, and now in the excitement of the moment he had exaggerated a little more than perhaps he should have. In fact he had more than doubled the number.

Joe continued. 'While we have others wanting to make the tank, we will supply ends, and I don't believe you will be able to stop us.'

John was thrown completely off balance. He had not thought of this possibility. Leonie had opened the oven door and the aroma of fresh biscuits filled the room. 'Staying for supper?' It was a statement of confidence that all was well in Joe's house.

'No, thank you.' John was up from his chair and out of the house in a few seconds, William and George after him. George looked back with a shrug.

The supper Joe and his family had that evening was the best they'd had in years.

Weeks went by, and they did not hear any more from John or William. The drought was still in progress and the Mooroopna Foundry was in danger of closing. Production of the tank ends had dwindled to just a few, and they had no other work. Ted's father had closed his butcher's shop and was now asking a small amount of rent. This didn't help, and now as so often before, Joe was gripped by uncertainty for the future. The sweetness of victory over John and his self-importance lost its edge as the family's anxiety grew.

Leonie had read an article entitled 'Westward-Ho', which asserted that Perth and its surrounding areas were the new boom regions in Australia. As was her way, she left the article on the table and mentioned it to her boys. She sowed a seed that over the next few days grew in the minds of Sam and Felix.

Two weeks later they had reluctantly told Ted of their intention to move to the West. In a way this suited Ted, for he knew his father needed to sell the property. He did not know, however, that the reason was that his father was broke.

The boys set sail in November 1896. They had saved well and each had over £300. Leonie wanted to go with them. 'Maybe one day we'll go too,' she said as they left, putting her arm around Joe. Joe didn't move away, and to the boys the sight of their parents thus linked left a lasting memory.

Hot Set

CHAPTER 25

Such is Life,
or Would it be Death?

KATE HAD TURNED the large manila envelope several times as she sat on the tramcar that would take her several blocks to her rooms. In February 1897 Melbourne was in the grip of its annual heatwave. That and the extra weight of the package and its contents had made her abandon her usual walk and take the tram. Because of its size the package could not be delivered to her home address. She had been notified to call at the GPO to take delivery.

She had torn open the corner and as expected saw that it was Joe's manuscript returned, all seven hundred and thirty pages. Surely this meant a rejection. They would have kept it if they had been going to publish. The Sydney publishers had been examining it for nearly twelve months now and her regular contact by mail had built up her hopes that its acceptance was imminent. On the other hand there might have been some need for minor alteration before the run to print.

Once off the tram she quickened her step until, in the

confines of her room, she found the covering letter inside. It was from A.G. Stephens, the *Bulletin's* literary editor. The neat paragraphs were spaced in such a way that it was tempting to look for the one that contained the message, usually in the middle or at the end. Controlling herself, she read from the beginning.

After mentioning some technicalities and financial matters, Stephens spoke of a backlog of editing, and the pressure on readers editing a manuscript of such length and style. The clear inference was either to abandon the work or reduce it further to no more than 450 pages. Stephens explained that the stories should begin, proceed, then finish without the distraction of ramble. Finally he attempted to soften the impact by referring to Joe's extensive knowledge of literature and philosophy and his mastery of scene and character.

The walls of Kate's room closed in on her. Joe's manuscript rested on her bosom as she lay back on the bed, the letter and envelope scattered. She cried, deep sobs that usually came with a more human sorrow. For her it was a mixture of both effort and failure, for it seemed she could not satisfy the one she loved with what she thought was her stronger passion, a skill she had honed that would make her apart from other women in Joe's eyes. Now she wondered if *Such Is Life* would drive them apart.

In the dead of night she lay awake. How would she break the news to Joe? Should she suggest he return to poetry and short stories for the *Bulletin*. Or play down the critique and response from Stephens, suggesting it just required further cuts and that she could help?

There was one other idea that came to her that night, silly as it seemed. Why not make two books out of one? There were so many stories running through *Such Is Life*. It might be possible. This, she thought, might suit Joe, for she knew he would be reluctant to cut the book further.

She decided that tomorrow she would contact a couple of local writers who were admirers of Joe's work. Now as she drifted into sleep the idea of two books sparked into a distant light. Her mind tossed with emotion. She saw Joe's sad face burdened with decision, her thoughts now turning into dream as sleep came upon her. Reaching, she touched Joe's moustache to tickle away the pain until she felt a surge of sensations. Then suddenly he was gone, rejecting her, or rejecting his own writing. She woke with a start, surprised that her fingers were crowding at the dampness around her pubic hair. She closed her eyes and again Joe's face with the sad blue eyes came to her with the crash of orgasm.

The discussions with one of the writers was very worthwhile. Kate felt more confident now. Her resolve to have Joe's book published had the support of an admired and established writer and that would make the publishers listen.

She wrote to Joe, telling him of Stephens' letter but not sending it for fear that he might dispose of it in some manner or other. She asked that he come to Melbourne for a while and put to him her idea of making two books out of the material.

CHAPTER 26

To the
West

O VER IN THE West the drought had not happened. Sam and Felix could not believe the prosperity that now surrounded them. Sam had found work in Fremantle, in a large foundry manufacturing parts for steamships. Felix worked as a clerk in a shipping office. They had kept in constant touch with Ted and through their correspondence revived the idea of starting their own foundry together again in the West, where they could manufacture a range of mining components, and even the water cart if they wished.

Ted arrived in Perth in 1898 and later that year a foundry commenced operations. It was to be known as the Furphy, Newby & Furphy Foundry. They were good times that followed for the three, Ted with his young wife from Victoria, Sam and Felix both engaged to marry pretty girls from the West.

Joe had little left for him in Shepparton. There was a vibrancy and culture about Melbourne and he was quick to respond to Kate's call. He did feel guilty, however, about leaving Leonie for such long periods. While she had showed no interest in his writing, or for that matter in his Melbourne forays, he felt uneasy about the separation of his literary life from hers, and had vowed to her that some day soon he would make it up to her.

It was a lonely period for Leonie, for now she was alone in Shepparton more often than not, the rest of her family having made the break. Her long letters to Sam expressed this loneliness, until he wrote and suggested that she and Joe should consider moving to the West too. At first it was an idea that played lightly on her mind, but it gathered weight when she remembered Joe's words, that he would make it up to her one day.

The thought of ending her loneliness by moving to the West came to fill her waking hours. She wrote frequently to her sons, trying to get a picture of their life there. Answering letters from Sam, and now Felix too, allowed her to build up a case for Perth that Joe could not resist. If he wouldn't go with her, she would go alone. The thought of it brightened her days. She could wait now till Joe returned home.

Those early weeks in Melbourne were frustrating for both Joe and Kate. Joe had not been convinced at first by Kate's idea, preferring that the complete story be again revised, but Kate had been quick to point out that it would require a major cut of words, a reduction of about half the contents, and that if that was not achievable then nothing would be published, and the best he could hope for would be a display of his manuscript at his local Mechanics' Institute for a period before it was relegated to the obscurity of storage.

There was another reason too, for Kate could see that Joe was no longer capable of extended writing periods. She had noticed that his memory for his characters could not be retained, let alone the thread of narrative. His eyes too were failing; glaucoma was gradually spreading its haze over his vision, recalling the ophthalmia he had suffered long ago in the Riverina, and perhaps his days of writing were numbered. Besides, she now had other things to do with her life. She had determined that this would be her last attempt, and now she would make her intention clear to Joe.

A week later Joe now had the two women in his life declaring their different but persuasive ultimatums. Kate's offer was that she work intensively for six months to complete the two manuscripts, providing she had his constant help. Leonie demanded that after this period he would move to the West to join her and his family for the rest of his life. It was a timely request, for now somehow his writing was no longer a pleasure. He experienced no struggle in accepting both of these, for there was really no alternative.

After the first few weeks of start and non-start, Kate found a solution to just how to divide the manuscript into two works, for there was a section on Rigby, a character that reappeared throughout. He had somewhat of a double life, a country squire and a romantic layabout. She even suggested the new book's name: *Rigby's Romance*.

As the next five months dragged on, Kate found Joe to be more morose than ever. His ability with words was still a source of wonder, but she began to find him more predictable, to the point where she was annoyed by a sarcasm that was no longer directed to those of the landed gentry but now to his own people, the very ones he had once made a stand for. She found herself devoting more time than she should to analysing her past infatuation. At the same time, they found that they became more disciplined in their approach to the job at hand. The writing became tedious to the point where somehow both knew that this was the final chapter in their lives together. But the task progressed well, and in the sixth month they were finished to the editing stage.

A small party had been arranged to celebrate the completion of two edited manuscripts. It was arranged to coincide with Joe's last night in Melbourne. He was troubled at again leaving *Such Is Life*, for this always seemed the way, never quite seeing it through. Kate assured him that within twelve months he would see the finished book.

The party was held at a Melbourne club, one that was largely comprised of artists and writers. It was a venue that Joe would never be invited to again, for he caused an embarrassment that would be remembered for many years, and for a long time afterwards those closest to him were still unsure why he did it.

He had arranged for Leonie to be invited to the party. She was surprised at the invitation, and not all that keen to attend, but Joe had insisted, explaining that this was their last week in Victoria. At the party Leonie had at first gone unnoticed. Her slight, bohemian looks fitted in with many of those present. It was when they were asked to be seated that the trouble occurred. Leonie had found the pre-dinner drinks hard going, to the extent that she wandered away from groups, politely but at the earliest convenient moment. Joe was aware of her unease and was secretly pleased that she had the gumption to move.

Leonie found herself alongside a dining table, and noticed Joe's place-name at the nearest setting. Expecting to see her own name alongside, she noticed another name, Kate. She quickly glanced to the other side and saw a man's name she didn't recognise. Instinctively she swapped her card with Kate's.

When they were invited to be seated Kate moved directly to her prearranged place, for this was the moment she had been waiting for, a place of honour alongside Joe, who was in the eyes of many already a celebrity. As she pulled at the chair another small but firm hand was on it too and quickly Leonie had seated herself. Kate was at first stunned at the aggressiveness, then embarrassed. She went to Joe and in a voice that carried like a grace before meals, explained that his wife Leonie had switched the name cards. She was standing to one side of Joe, her hand on the back of Leonie's chair. Joe responded in a slow, nonchalant voice. 'It's right that my wife is next to me,' then proceeded to lead the other guests by starting to eat the first course.

Kate was confounded and humiliated. The night was no longer hers. Strangely, Leonie became more at home as the evening drew on.

The weeks that followed were disciplined, but put a severe strain on Kate. She decided to finish the project as soon as possible. For Joe his time was now more precious in Shepparton, as he tried to carry out his promise to 'make it up' to his wife. Now that the boys were gone, husband and wife could not go on pretending that they lived separate lives. So they reached some accord, made few demands on each other, but had no hostility either.

They sailed to Western Australia in the early part of the new century. Joe had sold his cottage for a pleasing amount, and most of their possessions too. They had freighted their few essential items one month before.

Kate was glad to represent Joe and promote his works for with them was part of her life, a fading chapter, and their success would be some recompense for her selfless collaboration with her former lover.

Epilogue

In 1906 Joe and Leonie had settled in a small cottage in Swanbourne, a village four miles out of Perth and close to his sons, now both married and with children.

Such Is Life had been published in 1903 under the *nom de plume* of Tom Collins. The reviews were mixed, some claiming a masterpiece, others a 'real Australian yarn'. Others again asserted that its literary methods were poor, its powers of reproducing dialect phonetically mediocre. Sales were slow; it would only be after Joe's death that royalties would begin flowing.

In 1912 Joe was driving a horse and cart laden with heavy iron castings from Sam's foundry to a delivery point nearby. A slight rise had slowed the horse. Joe climbed down and walked beside it. Suddenly he felt pain in his chest. Not wanting to stop the horse, which was under stress too, he continued to the top of the hill then stopped. He moved to pat the animal's forehead; its nostrils were flared and red, its eyes wide with exhaustion and relief.

Another pain gripped at Joe, and as he fell to the ground he saw the broad face of a bullock, and the legs of the horse were transformed into the shorter, stronger leg of the great gentle creatures of his droving days. As he lapsed into a tunnel of unconsciousness there were layers of black shiny skin, wet with sweat, opening in front of him.

The load was now stationary, and Joe was dead.

John Furphy's foundry continued to flourish under the next generation, with William in charge. After the First World War, irrigation flowed through the surrounding areas. New machinery was invented for the changed agricultural circumstances and the foundry prospered because of it.

John moved to his wife's sister's house in Gardenvale, a southern suburb of the fast-growing city of Melbourne. Down here he was anonymous, just another face on the suburban block. In no time he had rectified that by becoming Grand Master of the newly formed Southern Masonic Lodge.

But the War was on everyone's minds. All were concerned for someone they knew. John was satisfied, for he had protected his sons from the call-up by becoming friendly with an influential past politician, who advised him on the wording required to apply for their exemption. It conveyed the possibility of manufacture of future army hardware. And it worked.

John died comfortably with many around him in his final moments, his mind in a spin of achievements, but unable to focus on any single one, for there was a darkness taking over. He was reaching out, desperate to hold on to just one moment, but it didn't come.

Author

Roger Furphy was born in Shepparton in 1940. He is the managing director of the Furphy Foundry which today manufactures street and park furniture, cast iron stoves and camp ovens. Roger Furphy's great-grandfather was John Furphy the creator of the water cart and many other pieces of farm machinery especially built for the Australian land. His great-grandfather's brother was Joseph Furphy, the writer of *Such is Life*, who described this work with the words: 'temper, democratic; bias, offensively Australian'. Roger Furphy lists among his pleasures, trout fishing and growing pine trees.

Engraver

William Hatherell, 1855–1928, besides being an excellent engraver was also an oil and water-colour painter of literary and historical figures. He had a strong reputation in England, America and Australia. These engravings were first printed in Cassell's four volumes of *Picturesque Australia*, 1890.

Two Brothers
by Roger Furphy

This book was wholly created in Australia
Printing and binding by Australian Print Group, Maryborough
On *Book Design* 120gsm and Cover *Conqueror Cream Laid* 220gsm from Jaeger
Design by De Luxe & Associates
Typeset in Janson by Patrice Hunt
Water cart drawing by Martin Wolterding
Wrestling arms drawing by James de Vries
Editing by Venetia Somerset
Editorial consultation from Neil Thomas
Engravings selection by Sarah Mattocks

First Edition : 2,000

ISBN 1 875368 29 9

We acknowledge some assistance from the Australia Council

Primavera Press
PO Box 575
Leichhardt 2040
Sydney Australia
telephone (61 2) 9569 1452
facsimile (61 2) 9564 1548

Publisher – Paul Brennan

This book may be ordered from the publisher but try your bookshop first.